Sophie Crampton is a barrister at Four Brick Court, specialising in care proceedings. She has been involved in a variety of complex matters such as cases involving children traveling unaccompanied from abroad, children and parents with significant physical or mental health needs and cases invoking the court's inherent jurisdiction. Sophie has extensive experience of drafting thresholds as well as challenging them and has recorded a webinar entitled 'Demystifying Threshold' with MBL seminars.

# Overcoming Threshold

## A Practical Guide to Threshold in Care Proceedings

# Overcoming Threshold
## A Practical Guide to Threshold in Care Proceedings

Sophie Crampton
Barrister
4 Brick Court

Law Brief Publishing

© Sophie Crampton

All rights reserved. No part of this publication may be reproduced, stored in a retrieval system, or transmitted, in any form or by any means, electronic, mechanical, photocopying, recording or otherwise, without the prior permission of the publisher.

Excerpts from judgments and statutes are Crown copyright. Any Crown Copyright material is reproduced with the permission of the Controller of OPSI and the Queen's Printer for Scotland. Some quotations may be licensed under the terms of the Open Government Licence (http://www.nationalarchives.gov.uk/doc/open-government-licence/version/3).

Cover image © iStockphoto.com/nuttiwut rodbangpong

The information in this book was believed to be correct at the time of writing. All content is for information purposes only and is not intended as legal advice. No liability is accepted by either the publisher or author for any errors or omissions (whether negligent or not) that it may contain. Professional advice should always be obtained before applying any information to particular circumstances.

Published 2022 by Law Brief Publishing, an imprint of Law Brief Publishing Ltd
30 The Parks
Minehead
Somerset
TA24 8BT

www.lawbriefpublishing.com

Paperback: 978-1-914608-26-1

# PREFACE

I would like to thank everyone who supported me in the preparation and publication of this book. In particular, I would like to thank my partner for patiently reading through the first draft, Justin Tadros for his willingness to discuss threshold issues with me, and my publishers for helping me bring this from an idea into print.

My practice at 4 Brick Court consists predominantly of care work. Through this work, it has become clear not only how important threshold is but also the lack of clear guidance in this area. I have been asked to draft numerous thresholds for local authorities and it is a very steep learning curve with the guidance in relation to threshold spread across multiple sources and case law. My aim in writing this book was to provide care practitioners with a comprehensive guide to threshold containing all the key law and principles relating to both the threshold test and drafting threshold.

Where the full judgment for a case is available on Bailli or the Supreme Court's website, the link to this is included within the footnotes. For a full list of the cases cited in each paragraph, please refer to the conclusion chapter. As of 4 July 2022, the law in this book is accurate and up to date, to the best of my knowledge.

Thank you for purchasing this book and I hope you find it useful.

*Sophie Crampton*
*July 2022*

# CONTENTS

| | | |
|---|---|---|
| **SECTION ONE – THRESHOLD ELEMENTS** | | 1 |
| Chapter One | What Is Threshold? | 3 |
| Chapter Two | Findings | 7 |
| Chapter Three | Re A | 13 |
| Chapter Four | Relevant Date | 19 |
| **SECTION TWO – HARM** | | 23 |
| Chapter Five | Significant Harm | 25 |
| Chapter Six | Risk of Future Harm | 31 |
| **SECTION THREE – ATTRIBUTING HARM** | | 37 |
| Chapter Seven | Causation | 39 |
| Chapter Eight | Beyond Parental Control and the Questions Around Causation | 43 |
| Chapter Nine | Care Given to the Child | 49 |
| Chapter Ten | Reasonable Care | 55 |

| | | |
|---|---|---|
| **SECTION FOUR – EVIDENCE** | | **59** |
| Chapter Eleven | Adult Witnesses | 61 |
| Chapter Twelve | Child Witnesses | 67 |
| Chapter Thirteen | Expert Evidence | 73 |
| Chapter Fourteen | Evidence Arising During Proceedings | 79 |
| **SECTION FIVE – PRACTICAL TIPS AND CONCLUSION** | | **83** |
| Chapter Fifteen | Practical Tips for Drafting and Responding to Threshold Findings | 85 |
| Chapter Sixteen | Practical Tips for Using Evidence When Drafting and Responding to Threshold | 93 |
| Chapter Seventeen | Conclusion | 101 |

# SECTION ONE

# THRESHOLD ELEMENTS

# CHAPTER ONE

# WHAT IS THRESHOLD?

The threshold test or 'threshold' is central to all care proceedings. Whether or not this test is established can make or break a local authority's case and substantially impact the options available to the court. Yet the importance of threshold is often overlooked in the course of proceedings and is frequently more complex than it first appears.

This book will consider the elements of threshold in detail and the evidence that can be relied on in support of threshold. The book is not intended to cover all the cases that have been decided about threshold but instead will focus on the key decisions that have been made in order to fully explain each threshold element. This book will also set out ten practical tips to bear in mind when drafting or responding to threshold. The final chapter of this book will summarise the preceding chapters, including a list of cases cited within each chapter.

By way of introduction, this chapter will provide a brief overview of what is meant by the term 'threshold' within care proceedings. To illustrate this, this chapter will break down threshold into its different elements, which will be explored in more detail in the rest of the book. Additionally, this chapter will explore the difference between the final threshold and the interim threshold as well as the distinction between threshold and the welfare stage of care proceedings. Lastly, this chapter will consider the ability of the local authority to withdraw proceedings when threshold is not met and the court's role in this process.

## The Threshold Test

Within care proceedings, if the local authority seek a final public law order, such as a supervision order or a care order in respect of a child, they must first satisfy the court that the test set out in section 31(2) of the Children Act 1989 is met.

This section states:

> *31(2) A court may only make a care order or supervision order if it is satisfied –*
>
> *(a) that the child concerned is suffering, or is likely to suffer, significant harm; and*
>
> *(b) that the harm, or likelihood of harm, is attributable to –*
>
> *(i) the care given to the child, or likely to be given to him if the order were not made, not being what it would be reasonable to expect a parent to give to him; or*
>
> *(ii) the child's being beyond parental control.*

This test is referred to as 'threshold' and threshold is said to be crossed once the local authority have satisfied the court that this test is met. This test essentially requires the court to be satisfied that;

1. The child is suffering or is likely to suffer harm (risk of future harm is considered further in Chapter 6)

2. The harm is significant (considered further in Chapter 5)

3. The harm or likelihood of harm is caused either by the care given to the child or the child being beyond parental control (Causation is considered further in Chapter 7, beyond parental control in Chapter 8 and the care given to the child in chapter 9)

4. Where the harm is caused by the care given to the child, the care given to the child must fall below or outside of the type and standard of care that it would be reasonable to expect a parent to give to the child (what is reasonable care is considered further in Chapter 10).

The local authority must satisfy the court that the child is suffering or likely to suffer significant harm at the relevant date. This is generally the date when the care proceedings were issued, though exceptions will be considered further in Chapter 4: Relevant Date. The burden of proving that threshold is crossed rests on the local authority. As per Lord Lloyd of Berwick in Re H [1995] UKHL 16[1], the word 'satisfied' is a neutral word, simply meaning 'to make up its mind'. It does not impose any particular burden of proof on the court. However, in order to satisfy the court that this test is met, the local authority will need to seek particular findings and this will be considered further in Chapter 2: Findings.

As care practitioners will be aware, crossing threshold does not mean that a care or supervision order will be made. The court must go on to consider where the child should live and what order, if any, is in the child's best interests. This is known as the welfare stage and is beyond the scope of this book. However, it is important to bear in mind that the decisions the courts have taken in relation to threshold have been made knowing there is a further safeguard for parents before any order is made.

Interim Threshold

While the majority of the case law in this book will focus on threshold at the end of proceedings ('the final threshold'), it is important not to overlook the interim threshold. The interim threshold must be crossed in order for the court to make interim public law orders and proceedings may be dismissed if the interim threshold is not met. The test for the interim threshold is contained in s38(2) of the Children Act 1989, which is set out below:

> *"A court shall not make an interim care order or interim supervision order under this section unless it is satisfied that there are reasonable grounds for believing that circumstances with respect to the child are as mentioned in section 31(2)."*

In contrast to the final threshold, the court does not have to be satisfied that the test under s31(2) of the Children Act 1989, set out above, is met. At this stage, the court only needs to have reasonable grounds to believe

---

[1] https://www.bailii.org/uk/cases/UKHL/1995/16.html

that the child is suffering or likely to suffer significant harm, attributable to one of the grounds set out in s31(2)(b). This acknowledges the fact that, at this stage, the local authority may need time to investigate their concerns and gather evidence before the final hearing. However, despite the lower threshold test, there is protection for parents when the court goes on to consider whether any interim orders should be made and if the children should be separated from their parents. It is these questions, rather than the interim threshold test, that are the focus of the majority of the case law surrounding interim orders. These questions form part of the welfare stage and, as such, are beyond the scope of this book.

## Withdrawing proceedings

If the local authority, having issued care proceedings, then determines that it is in the children's best interests to withdraw their application for public law orders, they will need permission from the court to do this. As set out by Hedley J at paragraph 36 of his judgment in the case of K and Ors (Children) [2011] EWHC 4031 (Fam)[2], the court must first determine whether they still need to hear evidence on whether threshold is met. If this is not needed, the court will consider whether, without hearing evidence, the court can conclude that it is unlikely that threshold will be met. If the answer is yes, then the local authority should be allowed to withdraw proceedings. If not, the court will need to consider whether withdrawing the proceedings is in the children's best interests.

## Conclusion

This chapter has provided an overview of what is meant by the term 'threshold' and the statutory test for threshold. The chapter has considered the essential elements of threshold, interim threshold, the welfare stage and withdrawal of proceedings. The following chapter considers threshold findings, in particular how these findings are relied on to establish threshold and the court's role in determining which findings are necessary.

---

[2] https://www.bailii.org/ew/cases/EWHC/Fam/2011/4031.html

# CHAPTER TWO

# FINDINGS

As mentioned in the previous chapter, to assist the court in determining whether the threshold is met, the local authority will seek particular findings. This chapter will consider the findings sought by the local authority and the standard of proof that must be met before a finding can be proved. The chapter will also explore the court's powers in relation to threshold findings and the courts' approach to the interim threshold. Lastly, this chapter will set out the distinction between findings and evidence and discuss the relationship between the two.

Findings and the standard of proof

Once all the evidence in proceedings has been gathered, the local authority will produce a document setting out the facts they allege are true in order to establish threshold. This is known as a final threshold document and the facts relied on are often referred to as 'the findings sought'. This document should set out each fact that the local authority relies on as well as the evidence in support of these facts. Each fact will need to be agreed by one or both parents or determined by the court. Where the court makes a determination on a fact, this is referred to as a finding or a finding of fact. The court will determine each fact on the balance of probabilities. In other words, if the court considers that it is more likely than not that a particular fact happened, then this is treated as having happened. As per the case of Re B (Care Proceedings: Standard of Proof) [2008] UKHL 35[3], this standard of proof remains the same regardless of the seriousness of the facts that the local authority are seeking to prove.

---

[3] https://www.bailii.org/uk/cases/UKHL/2008/35.html

## The powers of the court in relation to findings

Where some but not all of the facts within the local authority's threshold document have been agreed by the parents, the court has the power to determine whether these concessions are sufficient to cross threshold. If the parents have made sufficient concessions to cross threshold, the court can determine that a contested hearing is not required even if further findings are sought by the local authority. This was highlighted in the case of Re B (Agreed Findings of Fact) [1998] 2 FLR 968. On the other hand, the parents agreeing that threshold is crossed will not prevent the court from investigating serious disputed facts where it appears they will be relevant to other matters such as contact. This was emphasised by the Court of Appeal in the case of Re M (Threshold Criteria: Parental Concessions) [1999] 2 FLR 728. In this case, the parents appealed the Judge's decision to hold a contested hearing to determine whether the adoptive father had sexually abused the children. In dismissing the appeal, the Court of Appeal concluded that the finding sought in relation to sexual abuse was substantially different to the concessions the parents had made. The Court of Appeal were of the view that this finding, if found, would have an impact on the adoptive father's contact going forward and therefore, the Judge was right to conclude that a contesting hearing was required.

Similarly, the local authority agreeing with the parents not to pursue a particular finding does not prevent the court reopening this finding later. This was confirmed by the Court of Appeal in Re D (Child: Threshold Criteria) [2001] 1 FLR 274. In this case, the mother's first-born had been hospitalised after consuming a large quantity of medication. It was not known whether this had been deliberating administered by the mother or accidentally consumed by the child due to inadequate supervision. The local authority and the mother agreed threshold on the basis of inadequate supervision. However, without a clear determination of whether or not the mother deliberately administered the medication, mental health experts within proceedings were unable to reach a conclusion with regard to the mother's mental health. As a result, the Judge determined that this finding needed to be litigated. The Court of

Appeal upheld this decision and made clear that there was no principle of 'issue estoppel' within care proceedings.

Despite the Court of Appeal's view on issue estoppel, this principle has been relied on in cases where the parents seek to reopen old findings. The most recent case was that of RL v Nottinghamshire CC & Anor (Rev1) [2022] EWFC 13[4]. In this case, Mostyn J saw no reason why issue estoppel should not apply to family cases. He relied on Jackson LJ's reasoning in Re E (Children: Reopening Findings of Fact) [2019] EWCA Civ 1447, namely, that "there must be solid grounds for believing that the earlier findings require revisiting". The application before him was the mother's application to reopen findings, made in 2016, that her child had suffered non-accidental injuries. The mother argued that the child should be tested for Osteogenesis Imperfecta, as this was not explored in 2016. While Mostyn J acknowledged that testing practices for Osteogenesis Imperfecta had changed, he was not of the view that this would be a reason to reopen old findings unless the old practice was not only unsafe but 'completely and categorically wrong'. He dismissed the mother's appeal.

While, in the majority of cases, the basis of threshold will rest entirely on the findings sought by the local authority, the court does have the power to make additional or alternative findings. The court's ability to do this reflects the quasi-inquisitorial nature of care proceedings and allows judges some flexibility. This can be particularly useful where matters arise during the course of a final hearing that have not been previously anticipated. However, judges must have very good reasons for departing from the findings sought by the local authority. This was emphasised by Lord Justice Wall in the case of Re G and B (Fact-Finding Hearing) [2009] EWCA Civ 10[5]. He also emphasised that judges must allow the parties a fair opportunity to respond to any additional findings the court

---

[4] https://www.bailii.org/ew/cases/EWFC/HCJ/2022/13.html
[5] http://www.bailii.org/ew/cases/EWCA/Civ/2009/10.html

is considering. This approached was reaffirmed by the Court of Appeal in A (Children: Findings of Fact) (No 2) [2019] EWCA Civ 1947[6].

Interim threshold

Most of this chapter has focused on the final threshold document and the court's approach to threshold findings at the end of proceedings. However, the local authority must also have an interim threshold document (either as a separate document or within their application) in order to issue care proceedings. Generally, the court will not make findings on this document. If the court does make findings, these findings will rarely remain in place until the final hearing. This was emphasised by Mr Justice Moor at paragraph 34 of the judgment in G (children: fair hearing) [2019] EWCA Civ 126[7]. At paragraph 35 of his judgment, Mr Justice Moor highlighted that s38(2) does not require findings of fact to be made on the balance of probabilities whereas s31(2) does. Due to this difference in the required standard of proof, he concluded that any findings made at the interim stage cannot be relied on to establish that the final threshold is crossed. This judgment clearly set out that the practice of telling parents, either expressly or implicitly, that they will be stuck with any findings made at an interim stage is wrong.

Findings vs Evidence

The findings sought by the local authority are not to be confused with the evidence the local authority rely on to support these findings, though both will be present in a threshold document. For example, during the course of proceedings, the court may order hair strand testing of a parent, which is then positive for cocaine on or before the relevant date. The finding sought would be that parent's use of cocaine caused harm to the child or placed the child at risk of harm, either through exposure to the parent's usage or through neglect as a result of the parent's intoxication. The hair strand test result is then used as evidence to support that finding

---

[6] http://www.bailii.org/ew/cases/EWCA/Civ/2019/1947.html

[7] https://www.bailii.org/ew/cases/EWCA/Civ/2019/126.pdf

but is not by itself capable of showing the child is suffering or is likely to suffer significant harm.

The finding sought will have an impact on the quality of the evidence needed to support it. The more unusual the finding sought is, the better the evidence the court will need to find it proved. This was highlighted by Lord Nicholls of Birkenhead in Re H [1995] UKHL 16[8], which was discussed in the previous chapter. This was also emphasised by Lady Hale in Re S-B (Children) (Care Proceedings: Standard of Proof) [2009] UKSC 17[9]. She put it in this way "If an event is inherently improbable, it may take better evidence to persuade the judge that it has happened than would be required if the event were a commonplace"

Conclusion

This chapter has considered threshold findings and the court's discretion to add additional findings or reopen findings that were previously not pursued. The next chapter considers the leading case on threshold findings and how the local authority should plead their case in relation to threshold, namely, Re A (A Child) [2015] EWFC 11.

---

[8] https://www.bailii.org/uk/cases/UKHL/1995/16.html

[9] https://www.supremecourt.uk/cases/uksc-2009-0184.html

# CHAPTER THREE

# RE A

The judgment of Sir James Munby in the case of Re A (A Child) [2015] EWFC 11[10] (referred to as 'Re A' within this chapter) is the leading case concerning threshold. Within care proceedings, the term Re A compliant threshold is often used to describe a properly drafted threshold document that compiles with the principles set out in this case. This chapter will consider these principles in detail.

<u>The principles</u>

At paragraphs seven to seventeen of his judgment, Sir James Munby set out three fundamental principles in relation to threshold, which can be broadly summarised as follows;

1. Findings of fact must be based on evidence (including inferences that can properly be drawn from the evidence) and not on suspicion or speculation. This evidence should be primary, first-hand evidence where possible.

2. There needs to be a link between the facts relied upon by the local authority and the harm that they say the child has suffered or is at risk of suffering.

3. Society must be willing to tolerate very diverse standards of parenting, including the eccentric, the barely adequate and the inconsistent.

---

[10] https://www.bailii.org/cgi-bin/format.cgi?doc=/ew/cases/EWFC/HCJ/2015/11.html&query=Re+A+(A+Child)+.2015.+EWFC+11

## First Principle: Findings of fact must be based on evidence

Sir James Munby's first fundamental point can essentially be split into two points, and indeed was by Sir James Munby within his judgment. The first point is that threshold must rely on facts and the second point is that facts must be supported by evidence. This section will explore each of these points in turn.

### Threshold must rely on facts

The local authority must seek findings of fact that the court can establish are either proved or not proved. Therefore, the findings sought by the local authority should not contain words such as 'suspected', 'appears to have' etc. Statements such as X alleged that a parent did Y are unhelpful, as it is unclear whether the local authority are seeking to prove the allegation was made or whether they are seeking to prove that the allegation is true. In most cases, to establish that the child is suffering or is at risk of suffering significant harm, the local authority will need to prove that the allegation is true. Therefore, they must plead the allegation on the basis that it is true within their threshold.

As highlighted by Sir James Munby and discussed briefly in the previous chapter, facts need to be separated from evidence when pleading threshold. There will be times when the evidence the local authority are relying on will be someone else's opinion or allegation. However, within a threshold document, the fact they seek to establish should be clearly pleaded, followed by the evidence they seek to rely on. For example, if the local authority are seeking to prove that a parent has a mental health condition, they will frequently rely on an expert opinion. The expert may state something like "In my opinion, it is likely the parent is suffering from condition A, based on symptoms X, Y and Z". The local authority must therefore seek a finding that the parent has condition A, then rely on the expert opinion as evidence of this.

*Facts must be supported by evidence*

There must be evidence to support the facts alleged by the local authority. This can include expert evidence, where it is relevant to threshold, and this will be explored further in Chapter 13: Expert Evidence. Where witness evidence is relied on, this should be first-hand evidence where possible. Witness evidence will be considered in more detail in Chapter 11: Adult witnesses and Chapter 12: Child witnesses.

*Example*

To illustrate the two points explored above, consider the following example, which is a paragraph that could appear in a social work statement.

> "On 5 January 2023, a social worker attended the family home for an unannounced visit. The mother answered the door and the social worker suspected she was drunk. The social worker asked to see the children but the mother told her they were asleep, despite it being 11am. The home appeared dirty and cluttered."

Where something like this appears, the first question to consider is whether the social worker identified is the social worker who wrote the statement. If yes, then the local authority has their primary evidence, though it lacks detail. However, if the statement is referring to a different social worker, then this paragraph is hearsay and, as per Re A, the local authority should try to produce a statement directly from the social worker involved. The potential difficulties with calling witnesses other than the allocated social worker is explored further in Chapter 11: Adult witnesses.

For the purposes of this example, let us assume that the social worker who witnessed this incident is the allocated social worker and they remain the allocated social worker throughout proceedings. Therefore, the local authority will have primary evidence from a witness who will be available at the final hearing. However, this paragraph lacks detail and this presents difficulties in establishing the threshold facts. At present, the facts that can be established are limited to:

a) A social worker attended the family home on 5 January 2023 at 11am.

b) The mother was present in the family home.

c) The social worker spoke to the mother.

d) The mother said the children were asleep.

The remainder of the paragraph are the impressions formed by the social worker and are not facts. The social worker in question needs to provide more detail about why they suspected the mother was drunk (e.g. if the mother was slurring her words or smelt of alcohol) and why the home appeared dirty (i.e. what the home actually looked like when the social worker saw it). What the social worker actually observed, rather than the social worker's impressions, can then be used as evidence for threshold.

Second principle: There needs to be a link between the facts relied on and the harm suffered

The harm that the child is suffering or at risk of suffering must be linked to the parents' care or the child being beyond parental control. It is therefore important that any threshold facts that the local authority seek to rely on demonstrate or help to demonstrate this link. This can be overlooked, particularly in relation to domestic abuse or substance misuse, where the harm may seem obvious. This will be explored further in Chapter 7: Causation.

Within Re A, Sir Munby referred to the harm a child has suffered. However, the wording of s31(2) of the Children Act 1989 requires the child to currently be suffering or be at risk of suffering significant harm. Therefore, when linking the facts to the harm, it is crucial that this is harm that the child is currently suffering or would be at risk of suffering at the time when threshold is met. For further details, see the next chapter on the relevant date.

### Third principle: Society must be willing to tolerate diverse standards of parenting

As per Hedley J in Re L (Care: Threshold Criteria) [2006] EWCC 2 (Fam)[11]:

> *"society must be willing to tolerate very diverse standards of parenting, including the eccentric, the barely adequate and the inconsistent. It follows too that children will inevitably have both very different experiences of parenting and very unequal consequences flowing from it. It means that some children will experience disadvantage and harm, while others flourish in atmospheres of loving security and emotional stability. These are the consequences of our fallible humanity and it is not the provenance of the state to spare children all the consequences of defective parenting. In any event, it simply could not be done."*

This passage was quoted by Sir James Munby in his judgment and has been repeatedly referenced by multiple judges in various different care cases. At its core, this passage concerns the limits of state intervention and warns against social engineering. Practically, there are two ways to interpret this:

Firstly, as a reminder that the harm the child is suffering or is at risk of suffering should be significant. Where a child suffers harm but this falls short of significant harm, state intervention is not warranted. What is or can be significant harm is considered in more detail in Chapter 5: Significant harm.

Secondly, it also serves a reminder that the standard that parents should be compared to is that of a reasonable parent, not a perfect parent. Parents may not make the right choice in every situation but that does not mean they have fallen below the standard of care it would be

---

[11] https://www.bailii.org/ew/cases/EWCC/Fam/2006/2.html

reasonable to expect a parent to give a child. This is considered further in Chapter 10: Reasonable care.

## Conclusion

This chapter has provided a brief overview of the leading case of Re A (A Child) [2015] EWFC 11 and set out the key principles highlighted by this case. These principles will be explored in more detail within the relevant chapters of this book. The next chapter considers the relevant date at which threshold must be crossed, i.e. the date at which the child was said to be suffering or be at risk of suffering significant harm.

# CHAPTER FOUR

# RELEVANT DATE

The relevant date is the date that the court must use to determine whether or not threshold is met. In other words, this is the date at which the child must have been suffering or have been at risk of suffering significant harm in order for threshold to be crossed. While the relevant date will be simple to determine in most cases, it has the potential to be a very complex issue. This chapter will consider the case law surrounding the relevant date and how the relevant date may change following intervention by the local authority.

The relevant date and protective measures

As mentioned in Chapter 1: What is threshold, the relevant date in care proceedings will generally be the date that the local authority issued proceedings.

However, in accordance with Re M (A Minor) (Care Order: Threshold Conditions) [1994] 2 FLR 577 ('Re M'), the relevant date can also be the date when the local authority took protective action. To illustrate this, consider the facts of Re M. In Re M, the child's mother was murdered by the child's father in 1991 and the subject child went to live in foster care, while their siblings went to live with the mother's cousin. The mother's cousin felt unable to care for the subject child and in 1992, the local authority applied for a care order. By the final hearing, the mother's cousin was of the view she could care for the subject child and a dispute arose as to whether threshold was met. It was argued that threshold could not be met as, at the time proceedings were issued, the subject child was in foster care and no longer suffering significant harm. Lord Mackay, in his judgment, concluded that the relevant date was the date 'at which the local authority initiated the procedure for protection under the Act", namely, when the child moved to foster care.

Curiously, Lord Mackay's judgment envisaged that the protective measures taken by the local authority would remain the same from when they were first taken until the conclusion of proceedings, as happened in this case. However, this is not always the case. Frequently, before proceedings are issued, the local authority will protect the child under s20 of the Children Act 1989[12], police powers of protection or an Emergency Protection order. They will then apply for an interim care order when proceedings are issued and if this is granted, the child's legal status and nature of the protective measures in place will change. There are also cases where protective measures end during proceedings, for example if a child returns home. Even when this happens, it is now widely accepted that this does not alter the relevant date for the purposes of threshold. This is clear from the case of Re K (A child: Threshold findings) 2018 EWCA Civ 2044[13]. In this case, the Judge at first instance had concluded that threshold was not crossed because the child appeared to have done well in the mother's care during the course of proceedings. In allowing the appeal, the Court of Appeal accepted the arguments on behalf of the local authority and the Guardian that the Judge had conflated the test for threshold with the test for the welfare stage. Peter Jackson LJ concluded that the Judge had failed to focus on the relevant date, namely, the time when protective measures were put in place. In reaching this conclusion, he highlighted that evidence after the relevant date could only impact threshold to the extent that it shed light on the situation at the relevant date. This will be explored further in Chapter 14: Evidence arising during proceedings.

Despite this, Re M remains the foremost authority confirming that the relevant date can be established when protective measures are taken rather than when proceedings are issued. Lord Mackay's judgment also highlights two important principles in relation to protective measures, which are still relied on today. The first is that protective measures must

---

[12] Accommodation of the child by the local authority that the parents can object to and end at any time. Usually undertaken only with the parents' explicit consent

[13] https://www.bailii.org/ew/cases/EWCA/Civ/2018/2044.html

be continuous up to the date that proceedings are issued. If a child is accommodated under s20 of the Children Act 1989, subsequently returned to their parents and then the local authority issue proceedings, the local authority cannot claim that Re M applies. Secondly, the local authority must "[initiate] the procedure for protection under the Act" i.e. they must accommodate the child under some statutory authority, such as s20, rather than simply advising that the child goes to live somewhere else. This issue arose in the case of H-L (Children: Summary Dismissal of Care Proceedings) [2019] EWCA Civ 704[14]. This case involved injuries to a child, which medical professionals viewed as non-accidental. The injuries occurred in May 2018 but proceedings were not issued until August 2018. During that time, at the local authority's insistence, the child was in the care of her father. At one hearing in these proceedings, the local authority's counsel sought to argue that the relevant date was May 2018, relying on Re M. However, this argument was quickly abandoned in recognition of the fact that, since May 2018, the child had been in the care of a parent rather than in the care of the local authority.

This is not to say that Re M cannot apply where a child is placed with a friend or relative under s20. In this scenario, the friend or relative is essentially acting as a local authority foster carer and thus, the local authority are taking protective action under the Children Act 1989. However, Re M will not apply where the child moves to live with a friend or relative under a private family arrangement. In this case, it cannot be said that the local authority took protective action "under the Act", even if the private family arrangement was made on their advice. It is unwise for the local authority to do this in any event as the friend or relative will not have parental responsibility for the child. In contrast, under s20, the friend or relative would be able to exercise parental responsibility as an agent of the local authority.

---

[14] https://www.bailii.org/ew/cases/EWCA/Civ/2019/704.html

### Present or future harm

Threshold is always considered in the present or future, i.e. at the relevant date, what harm was the child suffering or at risk of suffering. If the child was suffering harm but this stopped before the relevant date, then this cannot be relied on for the purposes of threshold. This was stressed by Lord McFarlane at paragraph 58 of his judgment in the case of Re S & H-S (Children) [2018] EWCA Civ 1282[15]. In this case, the basis on which the local authority issued proceedings, namely, that the father had injured the children, was not proven and therefore, the mother argued that threshold had not been met. Interestingly, the mother's appeal was dismissed. Ultimately, the Court of Appeal found that there was sufficient evidence before the court that the child was suffering harm at the relevant date, albeit not the harm initially relied on by the local authority. This will be explored further in Chapter 14: Evidence arising during proceedings.

### Conclusion

This chapter explored the circumstances where the relevant date will be earlier than the date proceedings have been issued, as per Re M, as well as situations where Re M does not apply. Additionally, the chapter provided a brief overview of the need to establish that the child was suffering significant harm or was at risk of suffering significant harm at the relevant date, rather than before or after this date.

This chapter was the final chapter for section 1 of this book, which considers the basic principles of threshold and the guidance set out in Re A (A Child) [2015] EWFC 11. The next section will consider what is meant by harm in relation to threshold, beginning with the next chapter that explores the meaning of significant harm.

---

[15] https://www.bailii.org/ew/cases/EWCA/Civ/2018/1282.html

# SECTION TWO

# HARM

# CHAPTER FIVE

# SIGNIFICANT HARM

As mentioned previously within Section 1, threshold requires the court to be satisfied that a child is suffering or likely to suffer significant harm. This chapter will consider what is meant by the term 'significant harm', including specific examples of what does and does not constitute significant harm in case law. The chapter will also explore the court's approach to significant harm and how significant harm should be identified.

<u>The definition of significant harm</u>

Harm is defined by s31(9) of the Children Act 1989 as "ill-treatment or the impairment of health and development including, for example, impairment suffered from seeing or hearing the ill-treatment of another". Within the same section, health is defined as "physical or mental health" and development is defined as "physical, intellectual, emotional, social or behavioural development". This section also clarifies that ill-treatment covers sexual abuse and ill-treatment that is not physical.

Despite this comprehensive definition of harm, there is relatively little within the statute about what constitutes significant harm. The only clarification on how significant harm should be interpreted comes from section 31(10) of the Children Act 1989. Even then, this section merely states that "[a child's] health or development shall be compared with that which could reasonably be expected of a similar child". The section only considers significant harm in relation to a child's health or development. Further, this section gives no guidance on how far below the health or development of a similar child the subject child would have to be in order to have suffered significant harm.

The definition of significant harm and what constitutes significant harm has therefore become the subject of case law. In Re B [2013] UKSC 33[16] ('Re B') within her dissenting judgment at paragraph 185, Lady Hale defines significant harm as harm which is "considerable, noteworthy or important", relying on the dictionary definition of 'significant'.

In Re B, the Supreme Court Justices also cited with approval the judgment of Hedley J in the case of Re L (Care: Threshold Criteria) [2006] EWCC 2 (Fam)[17] ('Re L'). This case was mentioned in Chapter 3: Re A in relation to Hedley J's now well-known view, that "society must be willing to tolerate diverse standards of parenting". Within his judgment, this comment appears to have been made very much with significant harm in mind. At paragraph 51 of his judgment, he stressed that significant harm must be "something unusual; at least something more than the commonplace human failure or inadequacy".

Examples of what does not amount to significant harm

With the above definitions of significant harm in mind, consider two cases where significant harm was not found. The first is Re L, Hedley J's case mentioned above, and the second is Re AO (Care Proceedings) [2016] EWFC 36[18] ('Re AO').

Re L concerned parents with learning difficulties, whose children had been removed under emergency protection powers before the start of proceedings. They were removed following an allegation of physical chastisement, which the judge at the final hearing found was not proved. By the time of the hearing before Hedley J, the local authority instead relied on the following: the alleged history of domestic violence between the parents, the children's behaviour during contact sessions, and the fact that the children had significantly improved in foster care. The local authority were only able to rely on the latter two points to the extent they

---

[16] https://www.supremecourt.uk/cases/uksc-2013-0022.html
[17] https://www.bailii.org/ew/cases/EWCC/Fam/2006/2.html
[18] http://www.bailii.org/ew/cases/EWFC/HCJ/2016/36.html

were capable of proving the state of affairs at the relevant date. This will be discussed in more detail in Chapter 14: Evidence arising during proceedings. Having considered all the evidence, Hedley J concluded that the local authority had failed to prove that the children suffered significant harm. At paragraph 52 of his judgment, he commented that the children had undoubtably suffered harm and would likely suffer harm in the future. However, he was not satisfied that this was significant harm and therefore, he was not persuaded that this harm opened the gateway to state intervention.

In Re AO, the parents wanted the baby, AO, to be adopted in the UK rather than placed within her birth family in Hungary. The parents did not want their family in Hungary to know about AO and did not want AO to know about her origins. The local authority and the Guardian contended that, as a result of the parents' wishes, AO had suffered significant harm and was at risk of suffering significant harm in the future. The focus of this argument was that the parents' wishes deprived AO of the opportunity to live within her birth family and understand her birth culture. The parents contended that the threshold was not crossed as giving up a baby for adoption did not amount to significant harm. Baker J agreed with the parents' argument. At paragraph 19 of his judgment, he emphasised that the threshold is unlikely to be crossed in cases where the mother has notified the local authority in advance and made responsible plans to relinquish the baby. In relation to any harm suffered by the baby, Baker J considered that this will be diminished by the baby moving swiftly to another carer in a planned way and was therefore not significant. He then went on to consider if the mother's actions were reasonable and this will be explored further in Chapter 10: Reasonable Care.

An example of what does amount to significant harm

While there are numerous cases where the courts have determined that the harm suffered by the child does amount to significant harm, this chapter will focus on one particular example. This is the case of B and G

(Children) (No 2) [2015] EWFC 3 (14 January 2015)[19]. This case is significant as it is the first reported case to consider Female Genital Mutilation (FGM) within care proceedings in the UK. Ironically, given the title of this section, in this case Sir James Munby concluded that the child had not suffered significant harm as FGM had not taken place. Nonetheless, he went on to consider the question of whether FGM could amount to significant harm, given the significance of this issue within future proceedings. At paragraphs 7 and 8 of his judgment, Sir Munby explained that there are four types of FGM, as defined by the World Health Organisation. Types 1 and 2 involve removal, in part or in full, of parts of the genitalia. Type 3 involves the narrowing of the vaginal opening, for example sowing the vagina shut and this is referred to as infibulation. Type 4 refers to other harmful procedures carried out for non-medical purposes. Examples given are pricking, piercing, incising, scraping and cauterizing the genital area. At paragraph 10 of his judgment, Sir Munby considered Female Genital Mutilation Act 2003. This Act makes it a criminal offence to excise, infibulate or otherwise mutilate the whole or any part of a girl's labia majora, labia minora or clitoris, save for specific medical purposes as defined within the Act. As highlighted by Sir Munby, this Act criminalises types 1, 2 and 3 but only criminalises type 4 when it amounts to mutilation and this is not defined by the Act itself. Sir James Munby concluded that all types of FGM, whatever form it may take, will amount to significant harm. He went on to consider FGM in terms of the care provided to the child and this will be considered further in Chapter 10: Reasonable care.

<u>Cumulative harm</u>

The above focus on significant harm should not be taken as indicating that each finding sought by the local authority must by itself demonstrate significant harm. The court will consider all the findings sought by the local authority collectively to determine whether the child was suffering or was likely to suffer significant harm. However, where individual

---

[19] https://www.bailii.org/ew/cases/EWFC/HCJ/2015/3.html

findings only demonstrate harm, which is not significant harm, it must be clear how these findings cumulatively amount to significant harm.

Identifying harm

Regardless of whether the local authority are relying on a single event or cumulative behaviour, the court must be able to identify how the findings sought amount to significant harm. As observed by Lady Hale at paragraph 193(3) in her dissenting judgment in Re B, "The court should identify why and in what respects the harm is significant". This was echoed by Lord McFarlane at paragraph 57 of his judgment in the case of Re S & H-S (Children) [2018] EWCA Civ 1282[20], discussed in the previous chapter. In this case, Lord McFarlane made clear that when making a finding of harm, it is important that the court identifies whether the harm is significant harm or simply harm.

While not directly related to the question of whether or not the harm is significant, it is also worth noting the comments made by Lady Hale at paragraph 193(2) of her judgment in Re B. Lady Hale made clear that the courts must identify the type of harm that the child was suffering or was at risk of suffering as precisely as possible. This is noteworthy as it stresses the importance of identifying, within the threshold document, whether the harm alleged was physical, psychological, emotional etc. It is reasonable to conclude that the courts will find it easier to determine whether or not the harm suffered is significant when they know what type of harm is alleged.

Conclusion

This chapter has considered the definition of significant harm and the duty of the courts to identify the significant harm that the child was suffering or was at risk of suffering. The next chapter will focus on how the court determines whether or not a child is likely to suffer significant harm for the purposes of threshold.

---

[20] http://www.bailii.org/ew/cases/EWCA/Civ/2018/1282.html

# CHAPTER SIX

# RISK OF FUTURE HARM

As discussed previously, threshold requires the court to be satisfied that, at the relevant date, the child was suffering or was likely to suffer significant harm. In relation to a child who was suffering significant harm, this is relatively straightforward. If the facts relied on by the local authority establish that the child was suffering harm, the court will simply need to determine whether this amounts to significant harm. This was explored in the previous chapter. Whether the child was likely to suffer significant harm is a more difficult question and consequently, has been the subject of case law.

This chapter focuses on whether a child was likely to suffer significant harm and the evidence required by the court to determine this. This chapter will also consider how far in the future a risk of significant harm can be for the purposes of threshold.

The meaning of 'likely'

The case of Re H [1995] UKHL 16[21] ('Re H') established that 'likely' in the context of 'likely to suffer significant harm' does not mean 'more likely than not'. Instead, as per Lord Nicholls of Birkenhead, 'likely' means "a real possibility, a possibility that cannot sensibly be ignored having regard to the nature and gravity of the feared harm". This was further refined by Hale LJ (as she then was) in the case of Re C and B (Care Order: Future Harm) [2001] 1 FLR 611[22]. At paragraph 28 of her judgment, when considering whether there was a real possibility of future harm, Hale LJ emphasised that the seriousness of the alleged harm will play a role. She explained that while a small risk of really serious harm

---

[21] https://www.bailii.org/uk/cases/UKHL/1995/16.html
[22] https://www.bailii.org/ew/cases/EWCA/Civ/2000/3040.html

may be sufficient, for slight or minor harm the likelihood that it may occur will need to be much greater. She expressed the view that even a 'virtual certainty' of minor harm occurring may not necessary be enough to justify state intervention.

The factual basis for future harm

In Re H, Lord Nicholls of Birkenhead also emphasised that the 'real possibility' of future harm must have a factual basis and the case of Re H itself provides an illustration of this. In this case, the eldest child, who was not subject to care proceedings, claimed she had been sexually abused by her step-father. The local authority sought to establish threshold on the basis that the younger 3 children were likely to suffer significant harm as a result of the sexual abuse that the eldest child had allegedly suffered. The trial judge was not satisfied, on the balance of probabilities, that the eldest child had been sexually abused. Therefore, the judge did not feel able to conclude that the younger children were at risk of significant harm. The local authority appealed but the appeal was dismissed by the majority of the House of Lords. As outlined in Lord Nicholls' judgment, the Lords determined that the risk of significant harm needed to be based on more than a possibility or suspicion that the eldest child had suffered abuse. Therefore, as the sexual abuse of the eldest child had not been found on the balance of probabilities, this could not be relied on to establish that the younger children were likely to suffer significant harm. This reasoning has been cited with approval in several subsequent House of Lords and Supreme Court cases including: Lancashire v B [2000] 2 AC 147[23], Re O (Minors) (Care: Preliminary Hearing) [2003] UKHL 18[24], Re B (Care Proceedings: Standard of Proof) [2008] UKHL 35[25],

---

[23] https://www.bailii.org/uk/cases/UKHL/2000/16.html
[24] http://www.bailii.org/uk/cases/UKHL/2003/18.html
[25] https://www.bailii.org/uk/cases/UKHL/2008/35.html

Re S-B (Children) (Care Proceedings: Standard of Proof) [2009] UKSC 17[26] and, importantly, Re J (Children) [2013] UKSC 9[27] ('Re J').

To understand the importance of Re J and its distinction from other cases, it is worth first considering its facts. In Re J, the mother's first-born child, T-L, had suffered serious non-accidental injuries and ultimately died of asphyxia. The asphyxia was caused either deliberately or as a result of the child being taken into bed with the mother's then partner, SW. Previous care proceedings in 2006 concerning T-L's sibling, S, concluded that either the mother or SW was responsible for T-L injuries. Despite not knowing the identity of the perpetrator, the court was able to conclude that threshold had been crossed and that S was at risk of suffering significant harm. The court reached this conclusion on the basis that either the mother or SW was the perpetrator and the non-perpetrator had failed to protect T-L. S was subsequently adopted. The mother then had a further child by SW, referred as IJ. Prior to IJ's birth in 2009, the mother separated from SW and formed a relationship with a new partner, DW. DW had two children from a previous relationship, HJ and TJ. The local authority issued care proceedings in 2011 in respect of HJ, TJ and IJ, after finding out about the 2006 care proceedings.

The local authority conceded that threshold could only be met on the basis that the mother was a possible perpetrator of T-L's injuries. As highlighted by Lady Hale in paragraph 56 of her judgment, there were other findings in 2006 proceedings that the local authority might have relied on. For example, the mother's collusion with SW to prevent the court from identifying the perpetrator, her failure to protect T-L if SW was the perpetrator, or deliberately keeping T-L away from health professionals. However, the local authority's concession narrowed the focus of the proceedings to a single question that the judge was asked to determine. The question was "whether [the mother]'s inclusion in a pool of perpetrators in earlier proceedings involving a different child and a different relationship can form the basis of the threshold in relation to a

---

[26] https://www.supremecourt.uk/cases/uksc-2009-0184.html
[27] http://www.bailii.org/uk/cases/UKSC/2013/9.html

subsequent child in later proceedings". The judge ultimately determined that this could not form the basis of threshold because "the likelihood of significant harm requires reference to past facts, which have been proved on the balance of probabilities". In other words, the mother's inclusion in the pool of possible perpetrators of T-L's injuries was not sufficient to establish a real possibility of significant harm to HJ, TJ and IJ. The mother had not been found, on the balance of probabilities, to be the perpetrator of T-L's injuries and therefore, there was not a solid factual foundation on which to base the risk of future harm.

The Supreme Court supported the judge's reasoning, relying on the case of Re H. However, in doing so, they highlighted that this case was different from Re H as it had been confirmed that T-L had suffered harm, albeit that the perpetrator had not been identified. They therefore carefully considered the case law surrounding unknown or uncertain perpetrators and the impact of this on whether the child is likely to suffer future harm. As summarised in Lord Reed's judgment at paragraph 95, the threshold will not be crossed on the basis that a possible perpetrator of significant harm to child X is involved in the care of child Y. Threshold will only be crossed if all the possible perpetrators of significant harm to child X are involved in caring for child Y. For instance, had the mother and SW remained together, threshold could have been crossed in respect of IJ. This is because T-L was injured by either the mother or SW and, had they remained together, IJ would have been in the care of a perpetrator and therefore, likely to suffer significant harm. This will be explored further in Chapter 9: Care given to the child.

Timescales

As highlighted by Lady Hale in Re B [2013] UKSC 33[28], the Children Act 1989 does not impose time limits on when any future harm may occur. That said, as addressed by Lady Hale at paragraph 190 of her judgment, the further the harm is in the future, the harder it is for the court to predict whether it will occur. Consequently, she stressed that the likelihood of future harm must justify the court intervening now, as

---

[28] https://www.supremecourt.uk/cases/uksc-2013-0022.html

opposed to a later point when the harm either has occurred or is more certain.

Conclusion

This chapter considered how the court determines whether, at the relevant date, the child was "likely to suffer significant harm" and the evidence that should be relied on in establishing this. This chapter also highlighted that while the significant harm can occur at any point in the future, the risk of future harm must justify intervention now.

This section has dealt with s31(2)(a) of the Children Act 1989, namely, the harm the child was suffering or was likely to suffer at the relevant date. The next section will consider s31(2)(b) of the Children Act 1989, namely, the causes of harm required for the purposes of threshold and how these causes should be linked to the harm suffered.

# SECTION THREE

# ATTRIBUTING HARM

# CHAPTER SEVEN

# CAUSATION

In order for the threshold test to be established, the significant harm the child is suffering or is likely to suffer must be attributable to one of two 'limbs' contained in s31(2)(b) of the Children Act 1989. Section 31(2)(b)(i) relates to the care given or likely to be given to the child. This is known as the 'first limb' of the threshold test and will be explored further in chapters 9 and 10. Section 31(2)(b)(ii) relates to the child being beyond parental control. This is known as the 'second limb' of the threshold test, will be explored further in the next chapter. The order of these chapters was chosen due to the significant overlap between the case law on parental control and the issues of causation discussed in this chapter.

This chapter focuses on how causation should be established within the threshold test and how the term 'attributable to' has been interpreted by the courts for the purposes of threshold. The chapter will then highlight the importance of establishing causation for threshold as a whole.

The interpretation of 'attributable to'

The term 'attributable to' indicates that there must be a causal connection between the significant harm the child is suffering or is likely to suffer and either the first or second limb of the threshold test. This was highlighted by Lord Nicholas in the case of Lancashire v B [2000] 2 AC 147[29]. However, he stressed that neither limb of the threshold test has to be the sole cause of the significant harm. Instead, it is enough for the purposes of threshold that one of these limbs has contributed to the significant harm the child is suffering or is likely to suffer. Lord Nicholas also points out that it is not necessary to have a direct cause and effect

---

[29] https://www.bailii.org/uk/cases/UKHL/2000/16.html

relationship between either limb and the significant harm. He gives the example of a parent entrusting a child to the care of a third party, without checking the suitability of that party to care for the child. If the third party then abuses the child, the harm suffered by the child is attributable to the inadequate care of the parent, for not checking the third party's suitability, as well as the third party themselves.

This concept is frequently demonstrated in cases where the local authority allege that one parent has failed to protect the child from a perpetrator of abuse, be it the other parent or a third party. The significant harm to the child comes primarily from the perpetrator but the parent's failure to protect them from the abuse also contributes to that harm. However, there must be a causal link between the parent's actions or inactions in failing to protect the child and the harm the child is suffering or is at risk of suffering. This was stressed by the Court of Appeal in case of L-W (children) [2019] EWCA Civ 159[30]. This case concerned a child, L, who sustained a number of concerning bruises, which were considered to be non-accidental. The police investigated and found that there were four adults who had cared for L around the time of her injuries. These adults were the mother, the mother's partner GL, the father PW, and his partner LP. Each of these adults was considered as a possible perpetrator of L's injuries. At the fact-finding hearing, the Judge concluded that GL had caused these injuries. The Judge also found the mother had failed to protect L from GL, which was the subject of the appeal. The Court of Appeal ultimately allowed the mother's appeal, reaching the conclusion that there was no evidence in this case that could properly lead to a finding that the mother failed to protect L. At paragraph 43 of her judgment, King LJ highlighted the absence of a causal link between the facts relied on by the local authority and the risk of significant harm to the child. As an example, she considered one of the findings relied on by the local authority in asserting that the mother had failed to protect L. This was a finding that the mother had failed to promptly disclose to social services that GL had suggested not involving the GP, after the mother discovered L's injuries. King LJ pointed out that

---

[30] https://www.bailii.org/ew/cases/EWCA/Civ/2019/159.pdf

the mother ignored GL's suggestion and immediately sought medical attention for L. She emphasised that the mother's failure to inform social services of GL's suggestion in no way contributed to the significant harm suffered by L, particularly in light of the mother's positive action in seeking medical help.

Additionally, within her judgment, King LJ provided general guidance on how failure to protect should be approached and this will be considered in more detail in Chapter 9: Care given to the child.

## The importance of causation

As illustrated above, the significant harm that the child is suffering or is likely to suffer must be attributable to either the first or second limb of the threshold test. This sounds simple but is often overlooked when drafting the threshold document and can be a key point for those representing parents. For example, for a parent's substance misuse to be part of threshold, the local authority must demonstrate that, at the relevant date, the substance misuse was either causing or was likely to cause the child significant harm. If this cannot be established, for example because there is no evidence of the child being neglected or exposed to the parent's substance misuse, then the local authority's case on this point will fail.

## Conclusion

This chapter has considered the causal connection that must exist between the harm a child is suffering or is likely to suffer and either the first or second limb of the threshold test. The next chapter will consider the second limb of the threshold test, namely, whether the child is beyond parental control. In particular, the chapter will focus on the difficulty that the courts have faced in establishing a link between significant harm and the child being beyond parental control.

# CHAPTER EIGHT

# BEYOND PARENTAL CONTROL AND THE QUESTIONS AROUND CAUSATION

As mentioned in the previous chapter, the significant harm the child is suffering or likely to suffer must be attributable to one of two possible 'limbs' of the threshold test. This chapter will focus on the second limb pursuant to s31(2)(b)(ii) of the Children Act 1989, namely, the child being beyond parental control. The chapter will start by considering the meaning of 'beyond parental control' before exploring three cases that consider how significant harm should be attributed to beyond parental control.

Beyond Parental Control

For a child to be beyond parental control, as the name suggests, they must be beyond the control of their caregiver or caregivers. As highlighted by Stuart-White J in the case of M v Birmingham City Council [1994] 2 FLR 141, the term 'parental control' is not necessarily limited to the control exercised by the child's legal parent. For example, in this case, Stuart-White J considered that the mother's co-habitee, Mr P, was exercising a parental function for the child, despite not being the child's legal parent or guardian. Stuart-White J emphasised that Mr P must therefore be included when considering whether the child was beyond parental control.

Stuart-White J also formed the view that the court should consider whether the child is beyond the control of its current parent or caregiver rather than that of a reasonable parent or caregiver. However, it is worth noting that the case did not turn on this point and Stuart-White J declined to formally determine it.

## Causation in relation to Beyond Parental Control

A significant proportion of the case law concerning beyond parental control has focused on causation, specifically whether being beyond parental control can be attributed to the child suffering or being likely to suffer significant harm. This case law has focused on two main questions:

1. whether the child being beyond parental control needs to be a direct cause of their suffering or being likely to suffer significant harm; and

2. whether the child's parents or caregivers need to be at fault in some way for the child to be beyond parental control.

Set out below are the three key cases considering these questions. These cases are all first instances decisions and as such no case is capable of overriding the others.

*Re K (Post-Adoption Placement Breakdown) [2013] 1 FLR 1*[31] ('Re K')

Re K, as the title suggests, concerned an adopted child, identified as K, who became the subject of proceedings again with her adoptive parents. The local authority sought to establish that K was likely to suffer significant harm attributable to her being beyond parental control. It was agreed that K's behaviour had been difficult for her parents to manage and that she was beyond their control. However, there was a dispute between the local authority and the parents as to whether the parents were at fault for K being beyond parental control. Additionally, the expert psychologist in proceedings had concluded that the risk of significant harm to K came from her suffering a reactive attachment disorder, rather than being beyond parental control.

At paragraph 148 of his judgment, HHJ Bellamy considered the phrase 'attributable to' in threshold and its relationship to beyond parental control. He stressed that being beyond parental control does not have to

---

[31] https://www.bailii.org/ew/cases/EWHC/Fam/2012/4148.html

be the only cause of harm to a child, as long as it is a contributory cause. In expressing this view, he relied on the reasoning of Lord Nicholas in Lancashire v B [2000] 2 AC 147[32], which was explored in the previous chapter. At paragraph 149 of his judgment, he concluded that the harm the child is likely to suffer can be attributed to being beyond parental control, even if the risk of harm primarily comes from their disorder. Consequently, HHJ Bellamy concluded that the harm K was likely to suffer was attributable to her being beyond parental control. His reasoning can be explained in the following way. There may be cases, such as this one, where a child is likely to suffer significant harm as a result of a disorder rather than being beyond parental control. This disorder may also cause behaviour that puts the child beyond parental control. If it does, then being beyond parental control will contribute to the risk that the child will suffer significant harm, despite not being the main cause of that risk.

At paragraph 153 of his judgment, HHJ Bellamy considered whether the parents had to be at fault for K to be beyond parental control. He cited The Children Act 1989 Guidance and Regulations, as updated in 2008, which states that "it is immaterial who, if anyone, is to blame [for the child being beyond parental control]". He therefore concluded that the parents did not need to be at fault and that K was beyond parental control. HHJ Bellamy found that threshold was met and granted a care order in respect of K.

The decision to make a care order in respect of K was subsequently considered by the Court of Appeal in Re E (a child) [2012] EWCA Civ 1773[33]. The Court of Appeal allowed the appeal and replaced the care order with a wardship order. However, the Judge's determination in relation to beyond parental control was not appealed and so was not tested by the appellant court.

---

[32] https://www.bailii.org/uk/cases/UKHL/2000/16.html
[33] https://www.bailii.org/ew/cases/EWCA/Civ/2012/1773.html

### Re P [2016] EWFC B2 ('Re P')[34]

Re P was again a case where the child, T, had been adopted and proceedings were subsequently issued in respect of the adoptive parents. The local authority applied to withdraw proceedings as T was currently in hospital under s3 of the Mental Health Act 1983 and all parties agreed T should remain there. While it was agreed between the parties that the local authority should withdraw proceedings, there was a dispute over whether or not threshold had been met. In contrast to Re K, by the time of this hearing, the local authority were not arguing that the parents were at fault. They nonetheless contended that threshold was crossed on the basis that T was suffering or was likely to suffer significant harm attributable to her being beyond parental control. The local authority contended that whilst the harm T was suffering or was likely to suffer was caused by her mental health diagnosis, this harm was attributable, at least in part, to her being beyond parental control. They relied on the reasoning of HHJ Bellamy in Re K, set out above. HHJ Redgrave considered the ordinary construction of s31(2) of the Children Act 1989. She determined that this section requires some causal connection, however slight, between the harm the child is suffering or at risk of suffering and the child being beyond parental control. She disagreed with the reasoning of HHJ Bellamy in Re K and found the threshold had not been crossed.

In relation to fault, she noted HHJ Bellamy relied on the 2008 version of The Children Act 1989 Guidance and Regulations, set out above. She observed that the paragraph HHJ Bellamy cited has been omitted from the current version of the guidance. At the end of her judgment, she stressed that neither parent was in any way culpable for the behaviour of their daughter and the harm she has suffered or is at risk of suffering in the future.

---

[34] https://www.bailii.org/ew/cases/EWFC/OJ/2016/B2.html

T (A Child: Care Order: Beyond Parental Control: Deprivation of Liberty: Authority to Administer Medication) [2018] EWFC B1 ('Re T')[35]

In Re T, the child, T, had Autism Spectrum Disorder and severe learning difficulties. T displayed difficult behaviours, such as damaging property and the mother sought support from the local authority. The local authority provided support both at home and through respite provided by a specialist unit. By 2017, T was spending 6 days in the specialist unit and 4 days with his mother. Professionals formed the view he could not cope with these arrangements and that the mother was not implementing the advice of professionals when T was at home. T's challenging behaviours increased and the local authority issued proceedings in May 2017. The threshold was pleaded on the basis that T was beyond parental control and did not seek to assign any blame to the mother. This was supported by professional evidence that T's needs were beyond the capabilities of any reasonable parent and it would be extremely difficult to implement the required level of support in the community.

Recorder Darren Howe QC considered whether the parents need to be at fault for a child to be beyond parental control. At paragraphs 88 and 89 of his judgment, he stressed that beyond parental control was intended to be a no fault limb of threshold. He said to interpret it otherwise would undermine the ability of the local authority to protect children without embarking on a fault finding exercise. At paragraph 90 of his judgment, he stated that "it is immaterial whether a child is beyond parental control due to illness, impairment or for any other reason" and that the court's tasks is consider whether, on the facts, the child is beyond parental control. He explained that if the answer is yes, then the court goes on to consider whether the child is suffering or likely to suffer significant harm as a result of being beyond parental control. If the answer is also yes, then threshold has been satisfied.

On the facts of this case, Recorder Darren Howe QC found that T was beyond parental control due to his difficulties. He also concluded that,

---

[35] https://www.bailii.org/ew/cases/EWFC/OJ/2018/B1.html

due to T's difficulties, he was undoubtably suffering and at risk of suffering significant harm at the relevant date. He therefore concluded that the threshold had been met.

*The current position*

While the reasoning set out in the above cases may provide some guidance, the issues of fault and causation remain open for debate. In practice, beyond parental control is often pleaded as the 'no fault' limb of threshold and even within HHJ Redgrave's judgment, there is nothing that explicitly prohibits this. Her judgment focused on the absence of a causal connection between the harm the child was suffering or was at risk of suffering and the child being beyond parental control. Whether fault is required to establish this causal connection remains to be seen. Both Re K and Re T are quite clear that fault is not required. Instead, they suggest that being beyond parental control can contribute to the child suffering or being at risk of suffering significant harm, even if the primary cause of that harm is a medical condition or disorder. Both Re K and Re T also emphasis that a child can be beyond parental control as a result of their behaviour, irrespective of the cause of that behaviour.

Conclusion

This chapter has considered the second limb of the threshold test, beyond parental control, and outlined the debate in relation to how parental control should be linked to significant harm. The next chapter considers the first limb of threshold test, namely, the care given or likely to be given to the child.

# CHAPTER NINE

# CARE GIVEN TO THE CHILD

This chapter and the following chapter consider the first limb of the threshold test. In other words, these chapters will explore the part of the threshold test contained in s31(2)(b)(i) of the Children Act 1989, namely:

> *"the care given to the child, or likely to be given to him if the order were not made, not being what it would be reasonable to expect a parent to give to him."*

This chapter will provide an overview of this limb of the threshold test. Specifically, this chapter will focus on the identity of the caregiver, the importance of behaviour rather than intention, failure to protect, and what is meant by likely in this context. Chapter 10 will then go on to consider how the court determines the standard of care that would reasonably be expected of a parent.

## The identity of the caregiver

As confirmed by Lord Clyde in Lancashire v B [2000] 2 AC 147[36] ('Lancashire v B'), this limb of the threshold test does not specify who is providing care to the child. In other words, if the child is not receiving the standard of care that would reasonably be expected of a parent, it does not necessarily matter if that care is provided by a parent or someone else. In most cases, the identity of a child's caregiver will not be an issue as the local authority will be seeking findings against the parents in relation to the parents' actions or inactions. However, this issue does arise in cases

---

[36] https://www.bailii.org/uk/cases/UKHL/2000/16.html

where the child may have suffered harm outside the care of their parents. To illustrate this, let's consider the facts of Lancashire v B.

In this case, the child, A, sustained serious head injuries as a result of violent shaking on at least two occasions between September and November 1998. During that period, A's care was split between A's mother, A's father and a childminder. Ultimately, the Judge was unable to determine whether A's injuries were caused by A's mother, A's father or the childminder. The parents argued that the threshold could not be met as the court could not be certain that they were the perpetrators. However, on appeal, the Court of Appeal determined that the identity of the perpetrator was irrelevant for the purpose of threshold. A had suffered harm attributable to the care given to her and it did not matter which caregiver had caused that harm.

While this reasoning was approved by the House of Lords, they stressed that in most cases the threshold should relate to the parents or the child's primary carers. In his judgment, Lord Nicholls of Birkenhead said that the Court of Appeal's interpretation should only be applied in cases like this, where the child had been harmed by one caregiver but it was not possible to identity which caregiver had caused harm. This was echoed by Lady Hale in Re S-B (Children) (Care Proceedings: Standard of Proof) [2009] UKSC 17[37]. Lady Hale emphasised that this limb of the threshold test will not be met if a child is harmed at hospital, while at school or by a stranger, "unless it would have been reasonable to expect a parent to have prevented it".

Intention vs behaviour

The focus of this limb of threshold is the care given to the child or likely to be given to the child and whether this is reasonable. Thus, it focuses on the actions or inactions of the caregivers rather than what they may have intended. The parents do not need to have intended to cause significant harm to the child in order for this limb of the threshold test to be met. This was stressed by Lord Wilson at paragraph 31 of his

---

[37] https://www.supremecourt.uk/cases/uksc-2009-0184.html

judgment in Re B [2013] UKSC 33 ('Re B')[38]. This was also stressed by Lady Hale at paragraph 193(4) of her judgment within the same case. She emphasised that the harm must be "attributable to a lack, or likely lack, of parental care, not simply to the characters and personalities of both the child and her parents." She went to explain that "the court should identify the respects in which parental care is falling, or is likely to fall, short of what it would be reasonable to expect". In other words, the court must be able to identify something that the parents are doing or not doing, or are likely to do or not do, which impacts on the child's care. It is not enough for the parents to think or believe something unreasonable if this does not translate into action or inaction.

This concept works both ways, and it is possible for parents who are trying their hardest to still fall below the standard of care expected. This limb of threshold is not intended as a judgment on parents, who may be making the decision they think is best at the time. Cases involving unaccompanied asylum seeking children particularly demonstrate this concept. For example, consider the case of J (Child Refugees) [2017] EWFC 44[39], which concerned two children who arrived in the UK unaccompanied from Afghanistan. Peter Jackson LJ concluded that threshold was crossed as the children had suffered harm from "being sent across the world without any parental protection". At paragraph 15 of his judgment, he stressed that threshold is still met even though the children might have suffered worse harm if they stayed with their parents or caregivers.

Failure to protect

The importance of considering a parent's actions or inactions is perhaps best illustrated when considering the threshold finding of failure to protect. For example, consider the case of L-W (children) [2019] EWCA Civ 159[40], the facts of which were explored in Chapter 7. In this case,

---

[38] https://www.supremecourt.uk/cases/uksc-2013-0022.html

[39] https://www.bailii.org/ew/cases/EWFC/HCJ/2017/44.html

[40] https://www.bailii.org/ew/cases/EWCA/Civ/2019/159.pdf

King LJ did not make a finding of failure to protect against the mother as she had acted protectively by seeking medical attention for the child. In reaching this conclusion, King LJ stressed that a finding of failure to protect is a serious finding to make against a parent. She warned against considering these findings to be 'bolt ons' to the central issue of perpetration, particularly in cases where the parent remains living with the perpetrator of abuse. At paragraph 62 of her judgment, she provides examples of what will amount to failure to protect including covering up physical or sexual abuse or remaining in an abusive relationship where this causes the children emotional harm.

Failure to protect as a finding often arises, correctly or incorrectly, in what are known as 'uncertain perpetrator cases'. These are cases in which a child has been injured or indeed killed by one of their caregivers and the court is not able to identify, on the balance of probabilities, the perpetrator of the injuries. However, a finding of failure to protect against the non-perpetrator will not always be appropriate in these cases, particularly where the injury occurs during an isolated incident. This was emphasised by Lord Nicholls of Birkenhead in the case of Re O and N (Minors) (Care: Preliminary Hearing) [2003] UKHL 18[41]. Within his judgment, Lord Nicholls also stressed that a finding of failure to protect was not required for threshold to be crossed in these cases. In reaching this conclusion, he relied on the reasoning of the House of Lords in Lancashire v B, mentioned above, regarding the identity of the caregiver. Lord Nicholls considered that, as the threshold test does not specify the identity of the caregiver, threshold is crossed if the child has suffered harm and one of that child's caregivers was the possible perpetrator. He did not consider that it was necessary for the purposes of threshold for the child's other caregivers to have also been at fault by failing to protect the child.

For example, in Lancashire v B, discussed above, the Court of Appeal and the House of Lords were able to conclude that threshold was crossed as A had suffered harm attributable to the care given to her. Neither the

---

[41] http://www.bailii.org/uk/cases/UKHL/2003/18.html

Court of Appeal nor the House of Lords suggested that the parents, if they weren't the perpetrators, must have failed to protect A from the childminder. It was not necessary to do this in order for threshold to be crossed.

## Care likely to be given

As discussed in Chapter 6: Risk of future harm, it is possible for a child to be separated from their parents on the basis that they are likely to suffer significant harm. Where this happens before any significant harm has occurred, threshold will concern the care likely to be given to the child, rather than the care the child has actually received. The local authority will need to establish that the care likely to be given to the child would not meet the standard of care that would reasonably be expected of a parent. 'Likely' in this context means a 'real possibility' and the local authority must have a factual basis for making this assertion. This was explained in the judgment of Lord Nicholls of Birkenhead in Re H [1996] AC 563[42]. In Re B, mentioned above in relation to intention, Lady Hale emphasised that the parents' future behaviour will need to be considered. Specifically, she urged the court to consider how likely it is that "the parents' future behaviour will amount to a lack of reasonable parental care"

## Conclusion

This chapter provided an overview of the first limb of the threshold test and considered the circumstances where the care given to the child does not need to be provided by their parent. This chapter also highlighted the need to focus on the actions or inactions of parents and the need to approach the finding of failure to protect with caution. Finally, this chapter explored the meaning of 'likely' when considering the care likely to be given to a child.

The next chapter will focus on the meaning of 'reasonable' when considering the care given or likely to be given to a child, relying on

---

[42] https://www.bailii.org/uk/cases/UKHL/1995/16.html

examples from cases involving relinquished babies, FGM and children with disabilities.

# CHAPTER TEN

# REASONABLE CARE

The previous chapter provided an overview of the first limb of the threshold test. Specifically, it focused on the identity of the caregiver, the importance of behaviour rather than intention, failure to protect, and what is meant by 'likely'. This chapter will explore what is 'reasonable' when considering the care given or likely to be given to a child. To illustrate this, this chapter will consider the courts' decisions in cases involving FGM, relinquished babies and children with difficult needs.

What is reasonable?

Within the Children Act 1989, there is no definition of 'reasonable' or any explanation of the care that a parent is reasonably expected to give a child. What is reasonable and unreasonable will, to a certain extent, be defined through societal views that change over time. An example of this can be seen in the case of B and G (Children) (No 2) [2015] EWFC 3 (14 January 2015)[43], which was discussed in Chapter 5: Significant harm. In this case, Sir James Munby compared type 4 Female Genital Mutilation (FGM) with male circumcision. He concluded that both cause a child to suffer significant harm, with the difference being that male circumcision will always be an aspect of reasonable parenting, whereas FGM can never be. He explained that FGM has no religious or medical justification whereas male circumcision is often carried out for religious reasons and is regarded by some as being hygienic and protective. Thus, male circumcision is accepted by society as a reasonable parenting decision whereas FGM is not.

The importance of respecting reasonable parenting decisions has been emphasised throughout case law and particularly in cases where parents

---

[43] https://www.bailii.org/ew/cases/EWFC/HCJ/2015/3.html

have chosen to relinquish care of their child. For example, in Re AO (Care Proceedings) [2016] EWFC 36[44], also considered in Chapter 5: Significant harm, Baker J found that the parents had acted reasonably in giving up their baby for adoption. He stressed that while threshold is likely to be met in cases where a baby has been abandoned, it is unlikely to be met where a baby has been relinquished for adoption through appropriate channels.

## Children with significant needs

Threshold will not be crossed solely because the parents are struggling to meet their children's significant mental or physical health needs. This point was stressed by Hedley J in the case of K and Ors (Children) [2011] EWHC 4031 (Fam)[45]. This case concerned a family of 5 children, 3 of which had significant disabilities. Hedley J felt that there should be some model for what is or is not reasonable parenting in these cases and endeavoured to provide this. At paragraph 25 of his judgment, he explained that a reasonable parent must demonstrate commitment to meeting their child's needs. While a reasonable parent would accept the role of medicine, education, and social care in their children's lives, they do not always have to agree with the professionals for their behaviour to be reasonable. Indeed, he suggested that an overly compliant parent may not be behaving reasonably as they may not be displaying the necessary commitment to their child. Equally, at the other end of the scale, parents who refuse to engage with professionals or regularly reject professional advice may not be acting reasonably either.

In this case, Hedley J highlighted that the risk of significant harm experienced by the three children with disabilities was connected to their respective conditions and not to the care they were receiving from the parents. He expressed the view that these cases do not comfortably fit within the threshold criteria and generally should not enter the court

---

[44] http://www.bailii.org/ew/cases/EWFC/HCJ/2016/36.html

[45] K & Ors (Children), Re [2011] EWHC 4031 (Fam) (14 December 2011) (bailii.org)

arena. This view was endorsed by Hayden J in the case of Re W (A Child) [2021] EWHC 2844 (Fam)[46] ('Re W').

The case of Re W is significant for two reasons. Firstly, it exemplifies that a breakdown in the relationship between professionals and parents will not necessarily justify care proceedings. Secondly, it highlights that parents must not be held to a gold standard of behaviour. These points are best illustrated by considering the facts of this case. Re W concerned a child with very complex health needs, who required one to one care from a private care team. Care proceedings were issued by the local authority due to the parents' hostility towards the care team, which placed the child at risk of significant harm. However, a psychological assessment of the parents found that their responses were rational in light of the life-threatening medical events their child had experienced and the continuing uncertainty regarding their child's health. The psychologist commented that similar responses would be expected in "even the most psychologically robust person". Hayden J praised the psychologist for their report, which ultimately allowed the local authority and the parents to reach an agreement as to the way forward. At paragraphs 18 and 19 of his judgment, Hayden J considered s31(2)(b)(i) of the Children Act 1989, namely:

> *"the care given to the child, or likely to be given to him if the order were not made, not being what it would be reasonable to expect a parent to give to him."*

He specifically focused on the words "not being what it would be reasonable to expect a parent to give". Hayden J emphasised that this test must be looked at in the context of the difficult circumstances in which parents find themselves. He explained that when faced with a challenging situation, many people may respond in a way that seems objectively unreasonable. Hayden J stressed that parents must not be judged by a gold standard of parenting which few could achieve.

---

[46] https://www.bailii.org/ew/cases/EWHC/Fam/2021/2844.html

These cases stress that "society must be willing to tolerate diverse standards of parenting", which was the sentiment expressed by Hedley J in Re L (Care: Threshold Criteria) [2006] EWCC 2 (Fam)[47]. This case and Hedley J's views have been previously considered in both Chapters 3 and 5 of this book. It is a concept that is central to threshold and local authorities should be careful not to hold parents to impossible standards. Before issuing care proceedings on the grounds that the parents are not providing reasonable care, local authorities must consider what they would reasonably expect of a parent in that particular situation.

Conclusion

This chapter and the preceding chapter have provided a detailed look at the first limb of the threshold test, namely:

> *"the care given to the child, or likely to be given to him if the order were not made, not being what it would be reasonable to expect a parent to give to him."*

This chapter has focused on the meaning of 'reasonable' and highlighted the need to hold parents to a reasonable standard rather than a perfect one.

This section and the preceding section have taken an in depth look at the elements of the threshold test and what needs to be established to prove that threshold has been crossed. The next section will consider the evidence that can be relied on in order to establish that threshold has been crossed, known as evidence in support of threshold. The section will begin with the most common form of evidence used in establishing threshold, namely, adult witness evidence.

---

[47] https://www.bailii.org/ew/cases/EWCC/Fam/2006/2.html

# SECTION FOUR

# EVIDENCE

# CHAPTER ELEVEN

# ADULT WITNESSES

Witness evidence will often make up the majority of the evidence relied on in support of threshold. In accordance with Re A (A Child) [2015] EWFC 11[48], this witness evidence should be in the form of primary evidence. Primary evidence requires statements from witnesses who were actually present during the incident alleged and who are available for cross-examination if needed.

This chapter will outline the difficulties encountered when trying to obtain primary evidence from adult witnesses, including both professional and non-professional witnesses. This chapter will also consider hearsay evidence, including the case law and statutes surrounding the use of hearsay evidence in care proceedings. The next chapter will then consider the specific difficulties encountered with child witnesses and the use of ABE interviews as evidence.

Professional and non-professional witnesses

Where events have been witnessed directly by the allocated social worker, this provides good primary evidence from a witness who will be available at the final hearing. Theoretically, anything witnessed by a local authority social worker should provide good primary evidence in support of threshold. However, in reality, this may not be so straightforward. People's circumstances change and it is possible that between the incident and a statement being directed, the social worker will have left the employment of the local authority. Additionally, even if the local

---

[48] https://www.bailii.org/cgi-bin/format.cgi?doc=/ew/cases/EWFC/HCJ/2015/11.html&query=Re+A+(A+Child)+.2015.+EWFC+11

authority are able to obtain a statement, the relevant social worker may not be available to attend the final hearing to give evidence.

The situation becomes more complicated where the social worker's statement records things said to them by the parents or other significant caregivers. This can be primary evidence if the court is only interested in whether or not something was actually said to the social worker, such as where a parent makes a threat towards a child. However, if the court has to determine whether or not what was said was true, the social worker's evidence is unlikely to be enough.

Similarly, it is common for social work statements to refer to events witnessed by other people, which the social worker has not witnessed themselves. Again, the social worker's statement will not be primary evidence for these events. Where the event was witnessed by another professional, e.g. hospital staff or police, this problem is relatively easy to rectify. Primary evidence from the relevant source can be obtained in the form of a statement, notes or a report, even if it might take some time.

However, if the social worker was told something by a non-professional witness, this presents difficulties. For example, if the social worker's statement relies on an event witnessed by an anonymous informant or a member of the public. Members of the public or people who wish to remain anonymous are far less likely to want to give a statement or attend court to give evidence, which prevents primary evidence being obtained. Even if a statement can be obtained, there may be other difficulties with non-professional witnesses. For example, if a father tells the social worker that the mother beats the children. In this instance, if the father is involved in the court process, he will be able to provide a statement and will be available to give evidence. However, the father may not be a very reliable witness or may have other motives for saying what he said.

Hearsay

Where primary witness evidence is not available, then the local authority can consider whether hearsay evidence should be relied on. Section 2(a)(i) of The Children (Admissibility of Hearsay Evidence) Order 1993 states that, within family proceedings, evidence given in connection with the upbringing, maintenance or welfare of a child shall be admissible notwithstanding any rule of law relating to hearsay. Care proceedings are clearly family proceedings and any evidence relevant to threshold must be connected to the child's welfare. Therefore, hearsay evidence in relation to threshold is clearly admissible under this order.

As an aside, hearsay evidence to which The Children (Admissibility of Hearsay Evidence) Order 1993 does not apply can still be admissible. The rules governing this are set out in rules 23.2 to 23.6 of the Family Procedure Rules 2010 but consideration of this is beyond the scope of this book.

While hearsay evidence in relation to threshold is admissible, this should only be relied on as a last resort. The local authority must consider carefully whether to rely on a finding supported solely or primarily by hearsay evidence, particularly where that finding is likely to be disputed. This has been stressed by both the then president Sir James Munby in Re A (A Child) [2015] EWFC 11 and Aikens LJ in J (A Child) [2015] EWCA Civ 222[49].

In most cases, the local authority will need to be prepared to call witnesses to support the threshold findings they seek. This was emphasised by Black LJ in Re W (Fact-Finding Hearing: Hearsay Evidence) [2013] EWCA Civ 1374[50] ('Re W'). At paragraph 22 of her judgment, she stressed that where an adult's evidence is central to a finding sought by the local authority, it is expected that they will be available to give evidence if required. Black LJ then explained, at paragraph 24 of her judgment, that if a witness has difficulty giving evidence, special measures such as screens or the use of a videolink should be considered. If none of these measures can secure the attendance of a witness, the court will then go on to consider the reasons why the witness cannot give evidence or

---

[49] https://www.bailii.org/ew/cases/EWCA/Civ/2015/222.html
[50] https://www.bailii.org/ew/cases/EWCA/Civ/2013/1374.html

provide a statement. This will determine what weight, if any, should be attached to this evidence.

The above points made by Black LJ regarding witness attendance can be illustrated by considering the facts of Re W. In this case, the lower court made findings that T, who was an adult, and C, a child, were sexually abused by their father. The court also made findings that the mother knew about the sexual abuse of T and had failed to protect the children. These findings were challenged on appeal and are referred to in Black LJ's judgment as "the sexual abuse findings". In support of the sexual abuse findings, the local authority heavily relied on the account of T. T had been directed to file a statement but had not provided one by the time of the fact-finding hearing. T had depression and learning difficulties but it was not suggested that either of these prevented her from giving evidence or filing a statement. T had provided two letters in February 2013 and April 2013 retracting her allegations. At the beginning of May 2013, the social worker's statement stated that T was feeling under pressure from her family to write a statement supporting them. The social worker's statement said that T was not willing to provide a statement in relation to the abuse. In allowing the appeal, Black LJ noted that there was no evidence before the judge as to T's current position in June 2013, when the fact-finding hearing took place. Special measures to allow T to attend court or give evidence via videolink had also not been considered. Finally, Black LJ concluded that it was not apparent from the Judge's judgment that she had considered these factors in order to give the correct weight to T's evidence.

While primary evidence from a witness will usually be required, there may be situations where the local authority seek to rely on voluminous medical records or police disclosure. In those situations, calling the author of every report would be disproportionate and is unlikely to be possible. This was the case for the local authority in Westminster City Council v M, F and H [2017] EWHC 518 (Fam)[51]. In this case, the local authority sought findings in relation to the parents' behaviour towards

---

[51] https://www.bailii.org/ew/cases/EWHC/Fam/2017/518.html

hospital staff. They relied on allegations against the parents contained in hospital records for the child spanning several years. The court did hear evidence from the child's doctor as well as some of the nurses who had treated him but Hayden J concluded that the medical records should also form part of the evidential picture. He highlighted that this evidence was qualitatively different to witness statements and provides "contextual material by which the central evidential conflicts may be resolved". At paragraph 25 of his judgment, Hayden J helpfully summarised the approach to be taken to these records:

"The Local Authority must, ultimately, assess the manner in which it considers it can most efficiently, fairly and proportionately establish its case. The weight to be given to records, which may be disputed by the parents, will depend, along with other factors, on the Court's assessment of their credibility generally. Here, the reliability of the hearsay material may be tested in many ways e.g. do similar issues arise in the records of a variety of unconnected individuals? If so, that will plainly enhance their reliability. Is it likely that a particular professional e.g. nurse or doctor would not merely have inaccurately recorded what a parent said but noted the exact opposite of what it is contended was said? The reaction of witnesses (not just the parents), during the course of oral evidence, to recorded material which conflicts with their own account will also form a crucial aspect of this multifaceted evaluative exercise. At the conclusion of this forensic process, evidence can emerge and frequently does, which readily complies with the qualitative criterion emphasised in Re A ".

To summarise, the position in relation to hearsay evidence is that while it can be relied on in support of threshold, it shouldn't be relied on in most cases. Generally, the local authority should rely on witnesses able to give first hand evidence and consider the use of special measures to help witnesses attend court. Where this is not possible and hearsay evidence is relied upon, the local authority must carefully consider the weight that the court is likely to assign to this evidence. Where evidence comes from multiple independent professional sources, as in the case of medical evidence, hearsay evidence is likely to be more compelling than a statement from one source, particularly if they're anonymous.

## Conclusion

This chapter has considered witness evidence obtained from adults and when to rely on hearsay evidence from adults. The situation in relation to children is more complicated and will be explored in the next chapter.

# CHAPTER TWELVE

# CHILD WITNESSES

The local authority, the Guardian and other professionals will often report allegations made to them by children, who will usually be the subject of the proceedings. If these allegations are relied on as part of threshold, and are challenged by one or both parents, consideration will need to be given to whether the court hears evidence from the children themselves. This chapter will consider whether a child is able to give evidence and the factors to be taken into account when deciding whether they should give evidence. This chapter will also explore a key piece of hearsay evidence used in relation to children, namely, ABE interviews.

<u>Can children give evidence?</u>

The first question in relation to child witnesses is can the child give evidence? To determine this, the court will initially need to consider whether the child has sufficient understanding of the nature of the oath to give sworn evidence. If a child is not able to understand the nature of the oath, they may still be able to give unsworn evidence pursuant to s96 of the Children Act 1989. Under s96(2) of the Children Act 1989, a child's evidence can be heard by the court if in the court's opinion:

a) the child understands that it is his duty to speak the truth; and

b) the child has sufficient understanding to justify his evidence being heard.

Whether the child has sufficient understanding to give either unsworn evidence under s96 or sworn evidence will depend on the individual child and the evidence before the court in relation to their understanding. Expert evidence may be required in cases where the child has a mental health condition but is otherwise old enough and intelligent enough to have sufficient understanding.

## Should children give evidence?

Once it has been established that a child can give evidence, there remains the question of whether they should. The leading case in relation to whether children should give evidence in family proceedings is W (Children), Re (Rev 2) [2010] UKSC 12[52] ('Re W'). In her judgment, Lady Hale emphasised that the presumption against children giving evidence cannot be reconciled with the approach of the European Court of Human Rights. She highlighted that it is harmful to children if the court makes the wrong decision and needlessly separates them from their families or leaves them in abusive households. Therefore, the court should not ignore any relevant evidence that child witnesses may be able to provide. She concluded that the courts must weigh up two considerations when deciding whether to call a child as a witness. Lady Hale went on to provide guidance on how these considerations should be weighed up, setting out a number of factors that should be taken into account for each consideration. The two considerations and the factors to be taken into account are summarised below:

**First consideration: The advantages of the child's evidence in assisting the court to determine the truth.**

Factors to be taken into account:

- The issues the court has to decide to properly determine the case.
    - In other words, is determination of the allegation required to make a final decision or can the court reach a proper conclusion without this determination?

- The quality of any evidence the court already has before it.

---

[52] https://www.supremecourt.uk/cases/uksc-2010-0031.html

- The quality of any ABE interview conducted with the child (discussed later in this chapter).

- The nature of the challenges that parties wish to make to the child's evidence.

    o Lady Hale emphasised that the court is unlikely to be assisted by accusations that the child is lying. Equally, she expressed the view that the court will not be assisted by attempts to intimidate the child in cross-examination or a fishing expedition in the hopes something will turn up. However, she was of the view that the court may be assisted by focussed questions, which provide an alternative explanation for certain events.

- The age and maturity of the child.

- The length of time since the events in question.

- Any steps that can be taken to improve the quality of the child's evidence.

**Second consideration: The damage giving evidence will do to the welfare of the child.**

Factors to be taken into account:

- The age and maturity of the child.

- The length of time since the events in question.

- Any support the child has from family or other sources.

- The child's own wishes and feelings about giving evidence.

- - Lady Hale endorsed the view that a child who is unwilling to give evidence should rarely, if ever, be compelled to give evidence.

- The views of the Children's Guardian about the child giving evidence.

- Where appropriate, the views of anyone with parental responsibility for the child about the child giving evidence.

- The risk of further delay to the proceedings.

- Whether there are parallel criminal proceedings, which would involve the child giving evidence twice.

- General evidence of any harm that giving evidence may do to children.

- Any specific risks of harm to this particular child in giving evidence.

- Any steps which can be taken to decrease the risk of harm to the child.

Lady Hale emphasised that the court must be realistic in evaluating how to maximise the accuracy of the child's evidence while minimising the harm they may suffer from giving evidence. She highlighted that the court is not limited to traditional special measures or to traditional cross-examination. She gave examples of children being asked questions via videolink or via an intermediary, which can be the judge. Lady Hale predicted that, in most cases, the additional harm giving evidence will cause to the child will outweigh any benefits of the child giving evidence. Therefore, in most cases, children will not give evidence. However, she emphasised that this should be a conclusion reached by balancing the above factors rather than a hurdle that has to be crossed.

The above guidance must now be applied in any case where one party requires a child to give evidence. This is known as a Re W hearing. In light of Lady Hale's comments above, it is likely that in most cases the outcome of this hearing will be that the child is not called to give evidence. This means that the local authority will often be relying on hearsay evidence to support allegations made by children. This can be evidence from a social worker or the Children's Guardian on what was said to them but may also be in the form of a formal interview with the child. This is known as an ABE interview and will be explored further in the next section.

ABE interviews

ABE interviews are interviews conducted in accordance with the ABE guidance, entitled Achieving Best Evidence in Criminal Proceedings – Guidance on interviewing victims and witnesses, and guidance on using special measures (ABE) (March 2011). They are video-recorded interviews, usually carried out by the police with the assistance of an intermediary. ABE interviews are often relied on to support allegations made by children, particularly given that, as outlined above, children will rarely be called to give evidence to the court.

ABE interviews are not infallible and there will be instances where they are so flawed that the court cannot rely on them as evidence. An example of this is the case of Re W; Re F (Children) [2015] EWCA Civ 1300[53] ('Re W-F'). In this case, Baker J concluded that the judge at first instance was wrong to place any weight on the ABE interviews of L and M, two of the four children in proceedings. L and M were aged 4 and 8 respectively at the time of their interviews and both their interviews substantially breached the ABE guidance. An example of one of these breaches was that, in all of L's and M's interviews, the officer introduced or discussed the topic of abuse through leading questions. The judge had acknowledged that the approach to these interviews was shockingly poor but had nonetheless relied on what was said by the children within them. Baker J was of the view that, given the substantial breaches of the

---

[53] https://www.bailii.org/ew/cases/EWCA/Civ/2015/1300.html

guidance in this case, it was unsafe to rely on this evidence and allowed the appeal.

However, Re W-F is an extreme example containing very poor ABE interviews. Baker J's decision in this case should not be taken as indicating that any ABE interview that does not follow the guidance should be disregarded. Imperfectly conducted ABE interviews can still be relied on by a judge in reaching their decision, provided they are alive to the weaknesses in this evidence. To illustrate this, consider the case of Re M (A Child) [2010] EWCA Civ 1030[54] ('Re M'). Re M concerned an appeal by a father against findings that he had perpetrated sexually abusive behaviour towards three children. The basis of the father's appeal was that these allegations were supported solely by hearsay evidence. The father contended that the judge, while directing himself in relation to hearsay, had not followed this direction in reaching his decision. As part of his appeal, the father relied on the fact the children's ABE interviews had not meticulously followed the procedure laid down in the ABE guidance. One example relied on was that far too many interviews had been conducted with the eldest child. However, in dismissing the appeal, Hughes LJ made clear that the judge had considered the weaknesses of the evidence before the court and directed himself appropriately. Hughes LJ concluded that the judge was entitled to make the findings he did based on a holistic analysis of the evidence before him.

Conclusion

This chapter summarised how the court determines whether a child is capable of giving evidence and, if the child is capable of giving evidence, whether they should give evidence. The chapter also considered the use of ABE interviews to support allegations made by children, including when these interviews can be relied on as hearsay evidence.

The next chapter explores the use of expert evidence in care proceedings and how this can be helpful or unhelpful in terms of threshold.

---

[54] https://www.bailii.org/ew/cases/EWCA/Civ/2010/1030.html

# CHAPTER THIRTEEN

# EXPERT EVIDENCE

Expert evidence can be very valuable in establishing threshold. For example, in a non-accidental injury case, an expert's account of the child's injuries and their view as to whether the cause was non-accidental will be central to the proceedings. However, expert evidence will only be relevant to threshold where that evidence is linked to the situation at the relevant date. Most of the expert evidence gathered in care proceedings will therefore only be relevant to welfare issues, as the focus will be on the state of affairs after the relevant date.

This chapter explores two types of expert evidence commonly relied on in care proceedings, namely, mental health evidence and hair strand testing. For each type of expert evidence, the chapter will consider how this evidence can be relied on to support threshold, as well as the limitations of this evidence.

<u>Mental health assessments – psychological or psychiatric reports</u>

Mental health assessments, whether psychological or psychiatric, are commonly relied on as part of threshold to demonstrate that a parent has a diagnosis of (or symptoms consistent with) a particular mental health condition. However, in the absence of other evidence, this should not form part of threshold. A diagnosis alone does not establish that a parent has failed to provide the child with a reasonable standard of care or that the child has suffered harm. For threshold purposes, it is far more useful if the expert provides an opinion on the impact of a parent's symptoms or current behaviour on the child. This is more commonly considered within psychological reports, particularly reports of the whole family. The most helpful expert evidence comes from reports where the expert has interviewed the child directly. For example, a psychologist (Dr A) gives the view that a parent (Y) has symptoms consistent with Borderline Personality Disorder. They then assess the child (Z) and find that Z has a disordered attachment to Y. Dr A forms the view that this disordered attachment has negatively impacted Z's social development and contributed to their destructive behaviour. From their interview with Z and Y, they form the opinion that Y had been inconsistent in their emotional response to Z, as a result of their mental health. Dr A concludes that this would have contributed to Z's disordered attachment. For the purposes of the threshold, this would be plead as follows:

Y has mental health difficulties, which have impacted on Y's emotional response to Z. As a result, Z has suffered significant psychological harm. The local authority relies on the following:

a) Dr A formed the view that Y has symptoms consistent with Borderline Personality Disorder.

b) Dr A formed the view that Z has a disordered attachment to Y, which negatively impacts Z's social development and has contributed to Z's destructive behaviour.

c) Dr A formed the view that Y had an inconsistent emotional response to Z, due to their mental health difficulties.

d) Dr A formed the view that Y's inconsistent emotional response to Z would have contributed to Z's disordered attachment.

In the above example, there is no witness evidence showing that Y is providing an inconsistent emotional response to Z, it is solely based on the expert's opinion. Ideally, the local authority would also have examples of the parent's behaviour towards the child, such as behaviour witnessed by the social worker. The expert themselves may also have observed the parent and the child together and these observations can then be relied on as part of threshold. However, the expert's observations can only be relied on as part of threshold if they provide evidence of the situation at the relevant date, as discussed in the next chapter.

Establishing that an expert's observations or opinions relate to the relevant date can be problematic, particularly if the parent contends that their own or their child's mental health deteriorated after proceedings were issued. To establish whether a parent had mental health difficulties at the relevant date, the court would need to consider other evidence such as medical records or other professional records.

The expert's opinion may also have been formed by things said by the child during their interview. Where a child has made an accusation against the parent to the expert, and this is disputed by the parent, the court will have to determine whether to hear evidence from the child directly. This was considered in the previous chapter on Child witnesses.

Hair strand testing

Historically, hair strand testing has been treated as definitive evidence of a parent's drug or alcohol usage, elevating this testing to a level of unarguable fact. However, within the last decade, the courts have stressed that hair strand testing is a form of expert opinion and the experts themselves fully accept that this testing is not infallible.

This was explored in the leading case of London Borough of Richmond v B and others [2010] EWHC 2903 (Fam)[55]. This case was heard by Moylan J and concerned hair strand testing for alcohol. The court heard evidence from both a forensic toxicologist and a laboratory manager employed by TrichoTech, a hair strand testing company. Paragraphs 14-33 of Moylan J's judgment summarise the evidence heard regarding the hair strand testing process and how hair strand test results should be interpreted. This included an explanation of the agreed cut off levels used in hair strand testing, i.e. the minimum level of a substance that must be detected in the hair for the test to be positive. For the purpose of this chapter, the main points to be taken from this judgment can be summarised as follows:

---

[55] https://www.bailii.org/ew/cases/EWHC/Fam/2010/2903.html

1. Hair strand tests form part of the evidential picture but should not be used to form conclusions by themselves, in isolation of other evidence.

2. The markers used in hair strand tests for alcohol, namely EtG and FAEE, can occur naturally in the body or as a result of consuming things other than alcohol (for example some breads). Detection of these markers alone does not indicate alcohol consumption, which is why the cut off level for chronic excessive alcohol consumption has been agreed within field.

3. The agreed cut off levels for EtG and FAEE are for chronic excessive alcohol consumption only and there is no agreed cut off level for social drinking.

4. The testing is designed to establish a pattern of drinking over time and cannot indicate how much alcohol was drunk on one occasion or how frequently alcohol has been consumed.

5. The agreed cut off levels are said to be 'consistent with' chronic excessive alcohol consumption rather than proof of this consumption. Even relying on the generally agreed cut off levels, 10% of these results will be false positives.

The limitations of hair strand testing for drugs was considered in case of London Borough of Islington v M & R [2017] EWHC 364 (Fam)[56]. In this case, Hayden J acknowledged that hair strand testing for drugs is a well-established and uncontroversial practice but stressed that "hair strand testing should never be regarded as determinative or conclusive". He emphasised that hair strand testing must be consider within the broader evidential picture, including social work evidence, medical evidence and the individual's own account.

Both the cases mentioned above concluded that hair strand testing should not be considered in isolation. In order to provide reliable evidence of a

---

[56] https://www.bailii.org/ew/cases/EWHC/Fam/2017/364.html

parent's drug or alcohol usage, hair strand tests should always be supported by other evidence of the parent's intoxication e.g. witness evidence. This is particularly important where hair strand testing is relied on as part of threshold for two main reasons. Firstly, any hair strand testing conducted is likely to include a significant proportion of time after the relevant date. Therefore, other evidence will be needed to prove this drug use was occurring at the relevant rather than after the proceedings were issued. Secondly, for the threshold to be crossed, further evidence will be needed to demonstrate the impact of the parent's drug or alcohol usage on the child. For example, hair strand testing may show that a parent has been using cocaine for the past 6 months. Even if this includes the relevant date, the test by itself does not demonstrate that the child has been exposed to the parent's cocaine usage. To put this evidence in context and demonstrate the harm to the child, ideally there would be evidence of the parent being intoxicated around the child. At the very least, there would need to be evidence of the child being neglected, suffering harm or being at risk of harm in their parent's care. As explored in Chapter 7: Causation, a hair strand test result showing drug usage will not, by itself, establish threshold.

However, in light of the limitations of hair strand testing for alcohol in particular, the reverse is also true. If a parent does not meet the cut off level for chronic excessive alcohol consumption, this does not take away from other evidence showing that they were drunk while caring for the child. Just because the parent is not chronically excessively abusing alcohol, does not mean that the child is not suffering or is not at risk of suffering significant harm as a result of their parent's alcohol usage.

## Conclusion

This chapter has considered two types of expert evidence, mental health assessments and hair strand testing. The chapter explored how mental health assessments and hair strand testing can be relied on as part of threshold as well as the limitations of this expert evidence.

The next chapter will consider when evidence that arises after the relevant date may be relied on as part of threshold.

# CHAPTER FOURTEEN

# EVIDENCE ARISING DURING PROCEEDINGS

This chapter considers evidence arising after the relevant date and when this can be relied on as part of threshold. It sets out two types of evidence that can arise after the relevant date, namely, information and events. The chapter will then explore two cases where evidence arose during proceedings about harm the children had suffered that was not known about when proceedings were issued. For each case, this chapter will summarise court's determination regarding whether this evidence can be relied on as part of threshold.

<u>Types of evidence: Information and events</u>

To form part of threshold, information obtained after the relevant date must relate to things that happened around the relevant date. This includes reports from the child themselves about what was happening to them as well as expert reports, considered in the previous chapter.

After care proceedings have been issued, events can occur that demonstrate that one or both parents may be a risk to the child, for example, a parent being arrested for aggressive behaviour. These events can also be relied as part of threshold, providing that they relate to the parent's behaviour at the relevant date. This was confirmed in the case of Re G (Care proceedings: Threshold Conditions) [2001] 2 FLR 1111[57] ('Re G'). In this case, Hale LJ, as she then was, provided an example from her own experience of a baby suffering fractures. The baby was returned to the parents within proceedings and then suffered two new fractures.

---

[57] https://www.bailii.org/ew/cases/EWCA/Civ/2001/968.html

The new fractures were capable of being relied on as part of threshold as they related to the harm that the baby had suffered at the relevant date.

Information or events that do not relate to the relevant date cannot be relied on as part of threshold. That does not mean they should be ignored as they can be taken into account as part of the welfare stage.

### Evidence of harm not previously known about

In some cases, evidence will arise relating to harm that the local authority were not aware of at the time proceedings were issued. Whether this harm can be relied on as part of threshold was also explored in the case of Re G. Hale LJ concluded that this evidence could form part of threshold where it related to the relevant date. To explain this concept, let us consider the facts of Re G. In this case, the local authority issued proceedings on the basis of a cigarette burn, caused by the father. There was no suggestion of failure to protect by the mother and the father was in prison at the relevant date. It was clear that threshold could not be crossed on this basis, as the child was not suffering and was not at risk of suffering significant harm from the father. While the child was in foster care, several months after the proceedings were issued, the child's development improved significantly. Expert evidence was obtained, which concluded that the mother was unable to parent a child adequately to meet their changing needs. There was no evidence of any material change in the mother's parenting ability between the relevant date and the child's removal into foster care. However, the mother's parenting had not been a concern at the time that proceedings were issued. Hale LJ determined that, as the mother's parenting ability had not changed, the expert evidence related to the state of affairs at the relevant date. Consequently, she concluded that the expert evidence regarding the mother's parenting ability was capable of establishing threshold, even though there had been no concerns about the mother's parenting when proceedings were issued.

This approach has been affirmed in the case of Re S & H-S (Children) [2018] EWCA Civ 1282[58], mentioned previously in Chapter 4: Relevant Date. In this case, the local authority issued proceedings based on the father's physical chastisement of the children. However, during the course of proceedings, this was found not to have caused the children significant harm and the judge declined to make threshold findings against the father. The judge ultimately found that the threshold was crossed as the mother's mental health had caused the children to suffer significant emotional harm. The judge relied on a finding made in a previous set of proceedings regarding the mother's mental health and expert mental health evidence obtained in the current proceedings. The mother appealed. As part of her appeal, she relied on the fact that, at the relevant date, there were positive reports from professionals regarding her care of the children. She also argued that her mental health had deteriorated during the course of proceedings. The Court of Appeal determined that the previous finding and the expert evidence were sufficient to establish the mother's emotional and psychological vulnerability at the relevant date. Therefore, they concluded that the judge was entitled to find that threshold was crossed on this basis and dismissed the mother's appeal.

Both these cases demonstrate that the final threshold can be crossed based on significant harm that the child has suffered at the relevant date, despite the local authority not being aware of this harm when proceedings were issued. However, at paragraph 24 of her judgment in Re G, Hale LJ warned the local authority against issuing proceedings 'on a wing and a prayer' in the hope that evidence of harm will turn up. If they do, she made clear that the local authority open themselves up for a summary dismissal of their application and a judicial review of their decision to issue.

---

[58] https://www.bailii.org/ew/cases/EWCA/Civ/2018/1282.html

## Conclusion

This chapter has considered the information and events that can arise after the relevant date and when these can be relied on as part of threshold. The chapter also explored two cases where threshold was crossed based on harm that the children had suffered at the relevant date, even though the local authority were not aware of this harm when proceedings were issued.

This section has summarised the evidence that can be relied on as part of threshold and the key issues to consider in relation to different types of evidence. The next section will set out practical tips for drafting and responding to threshold, cross-referencing these tips with the rest of this book.

# SECTION FIVE

# PRACTICAL TIPS AND CONCLUSION

# CHAPTER FIFTEEN

# PRACTICAL TIPS FOR DRAFTING AND RESPONDING TO THRESHOLD FINDINGS

This chapter, along with the following chapter, will set out ten key practical tips that apply to both drafting and responding to the threshold document, drawing on the principles discussed in this book. The first five tips (in bold) relate to the threshold findings themselves and will be considered in this chapter. The last five tips relate to the evidence in support of these findings and will be considered in Chapter 16: Practical tips for using evidence when drafting and responding to threshold.

<u>Key practical tips</u>

**Threshold findings**

a) **Ask whether the findings are relevant to the threshold test**

b) **Consider the nature of the harm and its significance**

c) **Distinguish whether the harm has happened or is likely to happen**

d) **Keep the relevant date in mind**

e) **Consider causation**

Evidence

a) Distinguish between findings and evidence

b) Focus on facts

c) Look for primary evidence

d) Think about the reliability of evidence

e) Think about evidence early

**a) Ask whether the findings are relevant to the threshold test.**

Drafting

When drafting threshold, think carefully about how each of the findings sought relate back to the threshold test. Does the finding sought relate to one of the following:

i. the child suffering significant harm (or harm, if there is a cumulative effect);

ii. the child being likely to suffer significant harm;

iii. the child not being cared for in a way that it would be reasonable to expect a parent to care for them; or

iv. the child being beyond parental control.

If the answer to all of these is no, then this finding should not be included in the threshold document. To illustrate this, consider the following potential finding: "X (the parent) has not engaged with the local authority". Careful thought will need to be given as to how, if at all, this relates to the threshold test. For example, imagine there was a finding in previous care proceedings that X needs a high level of professional support to parent the child. This would connect the finding that 'X has not engaged with the local authority' to the threshold test by demonstrating that X has not engaged with the support required to parent their child. This allows the local authority to argue that the care X has provided, or is likely to provide, to the child falls below a reasonable standard of care. However, this argument should still be supported by other findings demonstrating how X's actions or inactions in caring for the child fall short of the standard of care that would be reasonably expected of a parent. Without a clear connection to the threshold test, it is unlikely that the finding "X has not engaged with the local authority" can be relied on as a threshold finding.

Responding

When writing a response to the threshold document on behalf of a parent, consider each of the findings that the local authority are seeking. Do these findings relate to the threshold test? All the findings sought should relate to the threshold test in some way and it should be clear from the threshold document how each finding relates to this test. Any findings that are either not relevant or are unclear should be removed or redrafted. It is worth asking the local authority to redraft the threshold document at an early stage in proceedings, to allow time for your client to respond to the redrafted document. If the local authority refuse, you can invite the court to order that the threshold document is redrafted. This will not only make the case against your client clearer but will avoid the risk of unnecessary findings being made against your client at the final hearing.

b) **Consider the nature of the harm and its significance.**

Drafting

As discussed in Chapter 5: Significant harm, judges must identify the nature of the harm that the child was suffering (or was at risk of suffering) at the relevant date. Additionally, judges must identify whether or not the harm the child was suffering or was at risk of suffering was significant. Setting out the nature and seriousness of the harm alleged within the threshold document will make the judge's task easier and is likely to make the local authority's case more persuasive. For example, consider the following finding: "the child was exposed to domestic abuse between the parents". This finding does not set out what harm, if any, the child has suffered, let alone if the harm is significant. For the purposes of threshold, it is much clearer to seek a finding such as "the child suffered significant emotional harm as a result of being exposed to domestic abuse between the parents". This clearly sets out the harm alleged and the fact that it is significant. This finding should be supported by examples of the alleged domestic abuse. These examples must demonstrate how the harm suffered is significant. Therefore, this finding should be supported by evidence of either a pattern of domestic abuse between the parents or a particularly serious incident that had an impact on the child.

<u>Responding</u>

As mentioned previously, when considering threshold, the court must identify the nature of the harm alleged and whether this harm is significant. Consequently, it is worth scrutinising the threshold document to ensure that this is clearly set out. If it isn't, it is worth asking the local authority to redraft their document or asking the court to order that the threshold document is redrafted. Not only does that give your client a clearer idea of the case they have to answer but also provides an opportunity to dispense with any findings that do not amount to significant harm.

> **c) Distinguish whether the harm has happened or is likely to happen.**

<u>Drafting</u>

The threshold document must make clear whether, at the relevant date, the alleged harm was harm that the child was suffering or harm that the child was likely to suffer. In practice, there is a lot of overlap between the two. Often findings will involve both types of harm as the child's situation at the relevant date will mean they are both suffering significant harm and likely to suffer future harm. However, as discussed in Chapter 6: Risk of future harm, this distinction becomes more important where threshold relies solely on the fact that the child is likely to suffer significant harm. For example, imagine child X has suffered harm but the local authority seek to establish that threshold is crossed in relation to child Y, who has not suffered harm. Child Y will not automatically be likely to suffer significant harm simply because it has been established that child X has suffered significant harm. The threshold document must clearly set out why there is a real possibility that child Y will suffer significant harm, relying on the situation as it was at the relevant date. There must be a factual basis for alleging that the harm that has happened to X will happen to Y or that there are specific risks of harm to Y. This may involve establishing that the situation has remained unchanged from the findings being made in relation to child X up to the relevant date in relation to child Y.

Responding

When responding to a threshold document, consider whether the local authority are seeking to establish that, at the relevant date, the child was either suffering significant harm or was likely to suffer significant harm. Where the local authority seek solely to establish that one or more children are likely to suffer significant harm, the findings relied on should be scrutinised carefully. The findings sought, if proved, must demonstrate that the risk that the child will suffer significant harm in the future is a real possibility rather than a 'mere suspicion'. This was discussed in detail in Chapter 6: Risk of future harm. For example, imagine a case where child X has suffered significant harm but the local authority seek to establish that threshold is crossed in relation to child Y, who has not suffered harm. Are the local authority relying on a parent of child Y being in a pool of perpetrators for child X? If so, are the caregivers for child Y the same as for child X? If not, as discussed in Chapter 6, then this finding by itself will not be sufficient to establish a real possibility of future harm to Y. Even if the caregivers have remained the same, have there been other changes in the caregivers' circumstances that would cast doubt on the possibility of harm to child Y? For example, if one of the caregivers has difficulties with anger management, have they accessed therapy to manage this? Where the local authority have failed to establish a real possibility of future harm, these findings should be taken out of the threshold document. As discussed previously, these findings can be removed either by the local authority agreeing to redraft the threshold document or by the court directing that the threshold document is redrafted. Where these findings constitute the local authority's entire threshold, you can apply for the proceedings to be dismissed on the basis that threshold is not met.

d) **Keep the relevant date in mind.**

Drafting

When drafting a threshold document, keep in mind the relevant date and consider how long before the relevant date a particular incident occurred. Very old but very serious incidents are worth including whereas less serious incidents should not be included unless they occurred close to the relevant date. Additionally, before including a particular finding, consider whether anything has changed between the incident relied on and the relevant date. As discussed in Chapter 4: Relevant date, to establish threshold a child must currently be suffering or be likely to suffer significant harm at the relevant date. Therefore, it is not worth including findings in relation to harm or likely harm that no longer existed at the relevant date. For example, if 5 years before the relevant date there was a serious incident of domestic violence, check whether the parents have since separated and whether the perpetrator still has contact with the children or the other parent. If the perpetrator has not been in contact with the family for some time, particularly if they are abroad or in prison, then the finding in relation to domestic violence will not be relevant to threshold. Equally, as explored in Chapter 14: Evidence arising during proceedings, incidents that occur after the relevant date will not be relevant to threshold unless they provide evidence of the situation at the relevant date. For example, imagine a parent enters into a relationship with a dangerous individual after the relevant date. This will not be relevant to threshold unless this is part of a pattern of behaviour, that existed at the relevant date, of exposing their children to dangerous individuals.

Responding

When responding to a threshold document, consider each finding sought in light of the relevant date. For example, does the threshold include historic incidents of neglect but the children were well cared for by the relevant date? Are there incidents of domestic abuse with a previous partner who, by the relevant date, no longer has any contact with your client? Equally, are there incidents of neglect or domestic abuse that occurred after the relevant date that do not link back to the situation at the relevant date? Findings relating to harm no longer present at the relevant date or harm that arose after the relevant date should not be included in the threshold document. This was discussed in more detail in Chapter 4: Relevant date and Chapter 14: Evidence arising during proceedings. As previously mentioned in this chapter, spotting findings like this and raising them with the local authority will be useful for your client going forward. Either the local authority will agree to remove them or the court can order that the threshold document is redrafted. Either way, the revised version of the threshold document should be easier for your client to respond to. Having a revised version of the threshold document will also avoid the risk that unnecessary findings will be made against your client at the final hearing.

e) **Consider causation.**

<u>Drafting</u>

Think about how the findings sought relate to each other. For example, findings that the subject child has suffered significant harm will only be relevant if they can be linked back to the parents' care or the child being beyond parental control. Equally, findings that relate to inadequate parenting will only be relevant if they can be linked to the harm the child was suffering or was likely to suffer at the relevant date. In this example, the inadequate parenting does not have to be the only cause of the harm to the child but must have contributed to it, as explored in Chapter 7: Causation. For instance, where a child has been assaulted by a third party, a parent's failure to seek medical assistance will not be the main cause of harm to the child but may contribute to it. However, the decision not to seek medical assistance will not be relevant to threshold if the child's injury did not require medical attention. Establishing a link between the harm a child was suffering or was at risk of suffering can be particularly complicated where the child is beyond parental control. This was discussed in Chapter 8: Beyond parental control and questions around causation. In these cases, careful thought will need to be given as to whether the harm the child suffered or was at risk of suffering is attributable to the child being beyond parental control. The case law discussed in Chapter 8 can provide some guidance on this, though the state of the law remains unclear.

## Responding

Consider how the findings sought by the local authority relate to each other. In particular, consider whether any findings in relation to significant harm are 'attributable to' either the parents' care or the child being beyond parental control and vice versa. The meaning of 'attributable to' was explored in detail in Chapter 7: Causation. As an example, imagine that the local authority are alleging that the parents misuse drugs. For the purposes of threshold, the local authority must establish that the parents' drug misuse contributed to the harm the child is suffering, or likely to suffer. If the local authority have not established this, then the finding in relation to the parents' drug misuse should be removed. If this is the only finding relied on by the local authority, it is possible to ask the court to dismiss the local authority's application on the basis that threshold is not met. If this is not the only finding relied on, then you can still seek for this finding to be removed, along with any other findings that do not establish a causal link. As mentioned throughout this chapter, this may be done voluntarily by the local authority or via a court order. This will trim down the number of findings your client has to respond to and avoid excessive findings being made at the final hearing.

## Conclusion

This chapter considered five practical tips concerning threshold findings, both for those drafting threshold documents and those responding to threshold documents. The next chapter will consider the evidence relied on in support of threshold. It will discuss five practical tips for evaluating the evidence relied on by the local authority, when both drafting and responding to the threshold document.

# CHAPTER SIXTEEN

# PRACTICAL TIPS FOR USING EVIDENCE WHEN DRAFTING AND RESPONDING TO THRESHOLD

The previous chapter considered five practical tips in relation to drafting or responding to threshold findings. This chapter will concentrate on the evidence relied on in support of threshold, including what evidence should be used and how this evidence should be used. These tips apply not only to those drafting the threshold document but also those responding to this document, by highlighting areas where it is worth questioning or challenging the local authority's use of evidence. Below is a list of the ten practical tips covered by this chapter and the previous chapter, with the tips covered by this chapter highlighted in bold.

Key Practical Tips

Threshold findings

a) Ask whether the findings are relevant to the threshold test

b) Consider the nature of the harm and its significance

c) Distinguish whether the harm has happened or is likely to happen

d) Keep the relevant date in mind

e) Consider causation

## Evidence

a)   **Distinguish between findings and evidence**

b)   **Focus on facts**

c)   **Look for primary evidence**

d)   **Think about the reliability of evidence**

e)   **Think about evidence early**

   a)   **Distinguish between findings and evidence.**

Drafting

When drafting the threshold document, it is important to set out what findings you are asking the court to make and the evidence that supports these findings. This can be difficult as findings and evidence are closely related. As an example, consider hair strand test results, which are often used in care proceedings. The threshold document may well contain a paragraph saying similar to the following:

> *"The parent tested positive for constituents and metabolites of cannabis during the approximate time period from the end of July 2022 to the end of October 2022. This indicates, on the balance of probabilities, cannabis use during that period".*

This is evidence and the threshold document should make clear that this is evidence. The finding sought would be "At the relevant date, the parent was using cannabis". Other findings should then be sought linking this cannabis use to the harm that the children are suffering or are likely to suffer, as discussed at point e) in the previous chapter.

## Responding

Before your client responds to the threshold document, it is important that the distinction between the findings sought and the evidence relied on has been clearly set out. If it hasn't, it is worth asking the local authority to redraft the threshold document or asking the court to order this. This will make it clear to your client what findings are being sought against them and make the threshold document easier to respond to. For example, imagine your client has been assessed by a psychologist as showing symptoms consistent with a diagnosis of depression. The local authority should set out whether they are seeking a finding that your client has depression or whether they are seeking a finding that your client has mental health vulnerabilities. Your client may agree that they have mental health vulnerabilities, even if they don't agree that they have depression. For findings that your client does not accept, a clear threshold document will also make it easier to consider the strength of the evidence relied on to support this finding. This will make it easier for you to advise your client on the strength of the local authority's case.

b) **Focus on facts.**

## Drafting

Social work statements and other local authority documents often include both facts and opinions. As discussed in Chapter 3: Re A, a threshold document should allow the court to determine whether each finding sought has been proven via reference to (mainly) factual evidence. Therefore, when drafting the threshold document on behalf of the local authority, it is important to separate out the relevant factual statements from the local authority's evidence. Where there are no factual statements to support an opinion, more information will be required. For example, a statement that says "the social worker suspected the parents' were intoxicated" will require more information about what the social worker actually observed. Did the parents slur their words? Was alcohol smelt on their breath?

Opinion evidence can be used where the person providing the opinion is an expert. For example, an expert psychiatrist offering their opinion on a parent's mental health. However, as explored in Chapter 13: Expert evidence, this evidence should be used with caution and only where relevant to the threshold test. Additionally, as with any other witness, where an expert is observing a parent's behaviour, their observations must be in the form of factual statements. For example, an expert psychiatrist can, based on their observations, offer an opinion on whether a parent is depressed. However, that opinion should be supported by factual statements regarding what the psychiatrist observed, what tests were carried etc, rather than merely giving their opinion without further detail.

Responding

When responding to the threshold document, focus on the facts that the parent needs to respond to. In relation to each fact relied on, a parent should be able to say whether or not something happened. Where the threshold document contains statements of opinion, consider whether these are statements from an expert offering an opinion on their area of expertise. Even if the expert is qualified to offer that opinion, it is worth looking at the expert report to see whether the basis for that opinion is clear. It is worth asking for the threshold document to be redrafted if it contains vague statements of opinion such as 'it was suspected that the parents' were intoxicated' or 'the accommodation appeared dirty'. This applies irrespective of whether the opinion is the opinion of a professional or an expert. As mentioned previously in this chapter as well as the preceding chapter, a properly redrafted threshold document will be easier for your client to respond to. This also limits the possibility of unexpected factual detail coming out at a later stage, such as in the witness box.

c) **Look for primary evidence.**

Drafting

As discussed in Chapter 3: Re A and Chapter 11: Adult witnesses, threshold findings should be supported by primary evidence where possible. For example, imagine seeking a finding that a parent has been aggressive in front of the child and relying on particular incidents where the police have been called. It is better to support this finding with police evidence from the incidents relied on rather than a second-hand summary of this information in the social worker's statement. The advantage of doing this is that it may provide further details about these incidents, allowing more specific threshold findings to be made. It may also be harder for the parent to dispute this finding where there are several first-hand reports from professionals there at the time. This may seem simple but is often overlooked, particularly where police disclosure has taken a long time to obtain or is incomplete. Equally, a finding that relies on something that someone else has witnessed, particularly if they are a non-professional, should be supported by a witness statement from that witness. If the witness is vulnerable or a child, this finding should still be supported by a detailed account from them, preferably in the form of an ABE interview. If there are difficulties getting an adult witness to attend court for the final hearing, consider whether there are any special measures the court could put in place to help them attend. This was discussed in Chapter 11: Adult witnesses. If the witness is a child, consider whether the child needs to attend court to give evidence, relying on the principles in W (Children), Re (Rev 2) [2010] UKSC 12. These principles were discussed in detail in Chapter 12: Child witnesses.

Responding

When responding to the threshold document on behalf of a parent, consider the evidence relied on by the local authority. As highlighted in Chapter 3: Re A, the evidence relied on should be primary evidence where possible. If it is not, it is worth asking the local authority to produce a report or witness statement from someone who was there at the time of the incident. This request should be made as early as possible to ensure this evidence is available in advance of the final hearing. This will have advantages when challenging this witness at the final hearing, as cross examination can be tailored to what the witness actually observed. Additionally, it separates that person's first-hand account from the account of the social worker or other local authority witnesses reporting it second-hand. Any inconsistencies between the primary evidence and the local authority's account can be highlighted and this may help eliminate any details that the local authority have misinterpreted or conflated with another source. If the local authority does not provide first-hand evidence, then arguments can be made at the final hearing about the difficulties of relying on hearsay evidence. Hearsay evidence and the weight to be attached to it were discussed in detail in Chapter 11: Adult witnesses. If the witness in question is a child, consider whether to ask for a Re W hearing. Re W hearings and the principles arising from the case of W (Children), Re (Rev 2) [2010] UKSC 12 were discussed in Chapter 12: Child witnesses.

d) **Think about the reliability of evidence.**

<u>Drafting</u>

When drafting the threshold document, it is important to bear in mind the reliability of evidence. This particularly applies to evidence from non-professional witnesses, who may have an ulterior motive for making allegations. This also applies to expert evidence, as discussed in Chapter 13. Even if the experts themselves are reliable, there are limits to the extent to which expert evidence can be relied on as part of threshold. For example, even if a parent's hair strand test shows a high concentration of cocaine in their hair, this only establishes that the parent uses cocaine. This cannot be relied on to conclude that the parent is a heavy cocaine user or has used large quantities of cocaine on a particular date. The limitations of hair strand testing were discussed in detail in Chapter 13 along with the limitations of mental health evidence for the purposes of threshold.

<u>Responding</u>

When responding to the threshold document on behalf of a parent, consider whether the evidence relied on in support of threshold is reliable. For example, an allegation made by another parent, particularly if they have chosen not to participate in the proceedings, can be easily challenged on the basis of reliability. In relation to expert evidence, the limitations of this evidence can be highlighted. For example, imagine the local authority are relying on the concentration of cannabis found in a parent's hair to say that they use cannabis in high quantities or throughout the day. It is known that the concentration of a drug in a person's hair sample does not equate to their level of usage, due to differences in individual metabolism rates. Most hair strand test reports now include a paragraph stating this. However, in the event this has not been included, questions can be put to the expert to clarify this point, in anticipation of challenging the local authority at the final hearing. Other limitations of hair strand testing and the limitations of mental health evidence are discussed in detail in Chapter 13: Expert evidence.

e) **Think about evidence early.**

<u>Drafting</u>

It is good to think about the evidence needed in support of threshold as early as possible. As highlighted in Chapter 11 and at point c) above, particular attention should be paid to any findings that currently rely on hearsay evidence. If there is anyone who can provide primary evidence to support these findings, this person or organisation should be approached as early as possible and a direction for this evidence obtained. If there is no one who can provide primary evidence for these findings, consider whether these findings should be pursued or abandoned due to a lack of evidence.

<u>Responding</u>

When responding to the threshold document on behalf of a parent, it is worth considering as early as possible what evidence the local authority are relying on. If the evidence relied on is unclear or primarily hearsay, the local authority can be asked to provide more detailed, first hand evidence, as discussed in point c) above. The advantage of this is that the parent will have a better understanding of the case against them and will be in a better position to challenge that evidence at the final hearing. If there are findings where there is no evidence or very little evidence to support them, it is useful to draw attention to this early. Hopefully, the local authority will then not pursue these findings at the final hearing. If these findings are pursued, then it can be highlighted to the court that the local authority were asked for further evidence in good time and failed to provide this.

## Conclusion

This chapter and the preceding chapter have set out ten key practical tips that apply both to drafting and responding to the threshold document. The next chapter will conclude this book by providing a summary of all the chapters in the book and a list of cases cited within each chapter.

# CHAPTER SEVENTEEN

# CONCLUSION

This book has considered the elements of threshold in detail, including how threshold should be pleaded in accordance with Re A (A Child) [2015] EWFC 11[59] and the evidence that can be relied on in support of threshold. This book also set out ten practical tips to bear in mind when drafting or responding to threshold. The following is a complete list of the chapters within this book, excluding this one, organised by section. Below each chapter title is a summary of the chapter's contents and a list of cases cited within that chapter. A link to the full judgment for each case will be provided in the footnotes, where available. To avoid confusion, each case will have its own footnote and the reader will be referred back to that footnote where cases have been cited in more than one chapter.

Section 1 – Threshold elements

Chapter 1 – What is threshold

This chapter provided an overview of the threshold test as contained in s31(2) of the Children Act 1989 and sets out the different elements of threshold discussed in this book. The chapter highlighted the distinction between the threshold test and what is known as the welfare stage of proceedings. It also detailed the interim threshold test as set out in s38(2). Lastly, the chapter considered the court's duties in relation to threshold where the local authority seek to withdraw proceedings.

---

[59] https://www.bailii.org/cgi-bin/format.cgi?doc=/ew/cases/EWFC/HCJ/2015/11.html&query=Re+A+(A+Child)+.2015.+EWFC+11

Cases cited in this chapter:

    i.    Re H [1995] UKHL 16[60]

    ii.    K and Ors (Children) [2011] EWHC 4031 (Fam)[61]

## Chapter 2 – Findings

This chapter described how threshold findings are used to prove threshold and set out the local authority's burden of proof in relation to these findings. The chapter also explained the standard of proof required for threshold findings and considered the court's approach to them, including at the interim threshold stage. Lastly, this chapter explored the relationship between the threshold findings sought and the evidence relied on in support of these findings. The chapter explained the need to clearly distinguish, within the threshold document, between the findings sought and the evidence relied on.

Cases cited in this chapter:

    i.    Re B (Care Proceedings: Standard of Proof) [2008] UKHL 35[62]

    ii.    Re B (Agreed Findings of Fact) [1998] 2 FLR 968

    iii.    Re M (Threshold Criteria: Parental Concessions) [1999] 2 FLR 728

    iv.    Re D (Child: Threshold Criteria) [2001] 1 FLR 274

    v.    RL v Nottinghamshire CC & Anor (Rev1) [2022] EWFC 13[63]

---

[60] https://www.bailii.org/uk/cases/UKHL/1995/16.html

[61] https://www.bailii.org/ew/cases/EWHC/Fam/2011/4031.html

[62] https://www.bailii.org/uk/cases/UKHL/2008/35.html

[63] https://www.bailii.org/ew/cases/EWFC/HCJ/2022/13.html

vi. Re G and B (Fact-Finding Hearing) [2009] EWCA Civ 10[64]

vii. A (Children: Findings of Fact) (No 2) [2019] EWCA Civ 1947[65]

viii. G (children: fair hearing) [2019] EWCA Civ 126[66]

ix. Re H [1995] UKHL 16[60]

x. Re S-B (Children) (Care Proceedings: Standard of Proof) [2009] UKSC 17[67]

Chapter 3 – Re A

This chapter concerned the principles set out by Sir James Munby in Re A (A Child) [2015] EWFC 11, the leading case in relation to threshold. The chapter considered each principle in detail, using examples to illustrate how these principles should be applied.

Cases cited in this chapter:

i. Re A (A Child) [2015] EWFC 11[59]

ii. Re L (Care: Threshold Criteria) [2006] EWCC 2 (Fam)[68]

Chapter 4 – Relevant date

This chapter explained the significance of the 'relevant date' in care proceedings. This included consideration of how the relevant date is generally worked out and the circumstances under which a different date will be used.

---

[64] http://www.bailii.org/ew/cases/EWCA/Civ/2009/10.html
[65] http://www.bailii.org/ew/cases/EWCA/Civ/2019/1947.html
[66] https://www.bailii.org/ew/cases/EWCA/Civ/2019/126.pdf
[67] https://www.supremecourt.uk/cases/uksc-2009-0184.html
[68] https://www.bailii.org/ew/cases/EWCC/Fam/2006/2.html

Cases cited by this chapter:

  i.   Re M (A Minor) (Care Order: Threshold Conditions) [1994] 2 FLR 577

  ii.  Re K (A child: Threshold findings) 2018 EWCA Civ 2044[69]

  iii. H-L (Children: Summary Dismissal of Care Proceedings) [2019] EWCA Civ 704[70]

  iv.  Re S & H-S (Children) [2018] EWCA Civ 1282[71]

## Section 2 – Harm

Chapter 5 – Significant Harm

This chapter explored the definition of significant harm, to the extent that this has been addressed by both statutes and case law. The chapter then went on to consider examples of what does and does not constitute significant harm. Lastly, this chapter set out the judicial approach to significant harm and the need to distinguish between harm and significant harm within the threshold document.

Cases cited by this chapter:

  i.   Re B [2013] UKSC 33[72]

  ii.  Re L (Care: Threshold Criteria) [2006] EWCC 2 (Fam)[68]

  iii. Re AO (Care Proceedings) [2016] EWFC 36[73]

---

[69] https://www.bailii.org/ew/cases/EWCA/Civ/2018/2044.html

[70] https://www.bailii.org/ew/cases/EWCA/Civ/2019/704.html

[71] https://www.bailii.org/ew/cases/EWCA/Civ/2018/1282.html

[72] https://www.supremecourt.uk/cases/uksc-2013-0022.html

[73] http://www.bailii.org/ew/cases/EWFC/HCJ/2016/36.html

# CONCLUSION

    iv.    B and G (Children) (No 2) [2015] EWFC 3 (14 January 2015)[74]

    v.    Re S & H-S (Children) [2018] EWCA Civ 1282[71]

## Chapter 6 – Risk of Future Harm

This chapter explained the meaning of 'likely' when considering whether a child is likely to suffer significant harm. The chapter also explored the evidence required within care proceedings to satisfy the court that the harm is likely. Lastly, this chapter considered how far in the future the likelihood of harm can be and the court's approach to this issue.

Cases cited by this chapter:

    i.    Re H [1995] UKHL 16[60]

    ii.    Re C and B (Care Order: Future Harm) [2001] 1 FLR 611[75]

    iii.    Lancashire v B [2000] 2 AC 147[76]

    iv.    Re O (Minors) (Care: Preliminary Hearing) [2003] UKHL 18[77]

    v.    Re B (Care Proceedings: Standard of Proof) [2008] UKHL 35[62]

    vi.    Re S-B (Children) (Care Proceedings: Standard of Proof) [2009] UKSC 17[67]

    vii.    Re J (Children) [2013] UKSC 9[78]

    viii.    Re B [2013] UKSC 33[72]

---

[74] https://www.bailii.org/ew/cases/EWFC/HCJ/2015/3.html
[75] https://www.bailii.org/ew/cases/EWCA/Civ/2000/3040.html
[76] https://www.bailii.org/uk/cases/UKHL/2000/16.html
[77] http://www.bailii.org/uk/cases/UKHL/2003/18.html
[78] http://www.bailii.org/uk/cases/UKSC/2013/9.html

OVERCOMING THRESHOLD

Section 3 – Attributing harm

Chapter 7 – Causation

This chapter explored how causation is established for the purposes of threshold, focusing specifically on the meaning of 'attributable to' within the threshold test. The chapter also highlighted why establishing causation is important and outlined the impact that overlooking causation can have on the local authority's case.

Cases cited by this chapter:

    i.    Lancashire v B [2000] 2 AC 147[76]

    ii.    L-W (children) [2019] EWCA Civ 159[79]

Chapter 8 – Beyond parental control and the questions around causation

This chapter explored what is meant by the term 'beyond parental control' within threshold and provided an overview of the current debate surrounding causation in relation to beyond parental control.

Cases cited by this chapter:

    i.    M v Birmingham City Council – [1994] 2 FLR 141

    ii.    Re K (Post-Adoption Placement Breakdown) [2013] 1 FLR 1[80]

    iii.    Re E (a child) [2012] EWCA Civ 1773[81]

    iv.    Re P [2016] EWFC B2[82]

---

[79] https://www.bailii.org/ew/cases/EWCA/Civ/2019/159.pdf
[80] https://www.bailii.org/ew/cases/EWHC/Fam/2012/4148.html
[81] https://www.bailii.org/ew/cases/EWCA/Civ/2012/1773.html
[82] https://www.bailii.org/ew/cases/EWFC/OJ/2016/B2.html

v.   T (A Child: Care Order: Beyond Parental Control: Deprivation of Liberty: Authority to Administer Medication) [2018] EWFC B1[83]

Chapter 9 – Care given to the child

This chapter focused on the significant harm caused or likely to be caused by the care given to the child. Specifically, it considered the identity of the person providing care to the child and the importance of their behaviour rather than their intentions. The chapter also considered what is meant by 'likely' when considering the care that the child is likely to be given.

Cases cited by this chapter:

i.   Lancashire v B [2000] 2 AC 147[76]

ii.  Re S-B (Children) (Care Proceedings: Standard of Proof) [2009] UKSC 17[67]

iii. Re B [2013] UKSC 33[72]

iv.  J (Child Refugees) [2017] EWFC 44[84]

v.   L-W (children) [2019] EWCA Civ 159[79]

vi.  Re O (Minors) (Care: Preliminary Hearing) [2003] UKHL 18[77]

vii. Re H [1996] AC 563[60]

Chapter 10 – Reasonable care

This chapter expanded on Chapter 9 by considering the definition of 'reasonable' in relation to threshold, focusing on how the courts determine if the care provided to the child is reasonable or unreasonable.

---

[83] https://www.bailii.org/ew/cases/EWFC/OJ/2018/B1.html
[84] https://www.bailii.org/ew/cases/EWFC/HCJ/2017/44.html

OVERCOMING THRESHOLD

This was illustrated using examples from case law, including cases involving FGM, children relinquished at birth and children with significant needs.

Cases cited by this chapter:

    i.    B and G (Children) (No 2) [2015] EWFC 3 (14 January 2015)[74]

    ii.    Re AO (Care Proceedings) [2016] EWFC 36[73]

    iii.    K and Ors (Children) [2011] EWHC 4031 (Fam)[61]

    iv.    Re W (A Child) [2021] EWHC 2844 (Fam)[85]

    v.    Re L (Care: Threshold Criteria) [2006] EWCC 2 (Fam)[68]

## Section 4 – Evidence

Chapter 11 – Adult witnesses

This chapter considered the challenges, illustrated with examples, that arise when relying on witness evidence in support of threshold. The chapter explored the difficulties with relying on professional and non-professional witnesses before considering hearsay evidence, pursuant to Section 2(a)(i) of The Children (Admissibility of Hearsay Evidence) Order 1993. This chapter provided an overview of the case law on hearsay evidence, highlighting the importance of relying on evidence from witnesses who have observed an incident first hand and are able to attend court.

Cases cited by this chapter:

    i.    Re A (A Child) [2015] EWFC 11[59]

---

[85] https://www.bailii.org/ew/cases/EWHC/Fam/2021/2844.html

ii.   J (A Child) [2015] EWCA Civ 222[86]

iii.  Re W (Fact-Finding Hearing: Hearsay Evidence) [2013] EWCA Civ 1374[87]

iv.   Westminster City Council v M, F and H [2017] EWHC 518 (Fam)[88]

Chapter 12 – Child witnesses

This chapter explored allegations made by children and reliance on children's evidence as part of threshold. The chapter considered the circumstances where children may give evidence as part of proceedings, including consideration of Re W and s96 of the Children Act 1989. Lastly, this chapter considered the use of ABE interviews with children as evidence within care proceedings.

Cases cited by this chapter:

i.    W (Children), Re (Rev 2) [2010] UKSC 12[89]

ii.   Re W; Re F (Children) [2015] EWCA Civ 1300[90]

iii.  Re M (A Child) [2010] EWCA Civ 1030[91]

Chapter 13 – Expert evidence

This chapter considered the use of expert evidence in support of threshold. In particular, it explored when hair strand testing and mental

---

[86] https://www.bailii.org/ew/cases/EWCA/Civ/2015/222.html
[87] https://www.bailii.org/ew/cases/EWCA/Civ/2013/1374.html
[88] https://www.bailii.org/ew/cases/EWHC/Fam/2017/518.html
[89] https://www.supremecourt.uk/cases/uksc-2010-0031.html
[90] https://www.bailii.org/ew/cases/EWCA/Civ/2015/1300.html
[91] https://www.bailii.org/ew/cases/EWCA/Civ/2010/1030.html

health evidence can and cannot be used as evidence in support of threshold. This was illustrated with examples and guidance from case law.

Cases cited by this chapter:

i. London Borough of Richmond v B and others [2010] EWHC 2903 (Fam)[92]

ii. London Borough of Islington v M & R [2017] EWHC 364 (Fam)[93]

Chapter 14 – Evidence arising during proceedings

This chapter set out when evidence obtained after the relevant date (usually after proceedings have started) can be relied on as part of threshold. The chapter distinguished between information relating to the relevant date that is obtained during proceedings and new events that occur following the relevant date. This chapter then explored the court's approach to cases where evidence arises during proceedings concerning harm, or a likelihood of harm, that was not known about when proceedings were issued. This approach was illustrated by the considering key examples from case law, including the leading case of Re G.

Cases cited by this chapter:

i. Re G (Care proceedings: Threshold Conditions) [2001] 2 FLR 1111[94]

ii. Re S & H-S (Children) [2018] EWCA Civ 1282[71]

---

[92] https://www.bailii.org/ew/cases/EWHC/Fam/2010/2903.html

[93] https://www.bailii.org/ew/cases/EWHC/Fam/2017/364.html

[94] https://www.bailii.org/ew/cases/EWCA/Civ/2001/968.html

## Section 5 – Practical tips and Conclusion

### Chapter 15 – Practical tips for drafting and responding to threshold findings

This chapter provided five practical tips for drafting and responding to threshold, with detailed explanations and examples. The chapter focused on the threshold test and the issues to bear in mind when either drafting or responding to a threshold document. Each tip was based on information discussed previously in this book and references to earlier chapters were provided where applicable.

### Chapter 16 – Practical tips for using evidence when drafting and responding to threshold

Like the previous chapter, this chapter provided five practical tips for drafting and responding to threshold, with detailed explanations and examples. However, this chapter focused on the evidence relied on to support threshold and provided practical tips for scrutinising this evidence. Each tip was based on information discussed previously in this book and references to earlier chapters were provided where applicable.

This chapter concludes Overcoming Threshold: A practical guide to threshold in care proceedings. Thank you for reading.

# MORE BOOKS BY LAW BRIEF PUBLISHING

A selection of our other titles available now:-

| |
|---|
| 'A Practical Guide to Parental Alienation in Private and Public Law Children Cases' by Sam King QC & Frankie Shama |
| 'Contested Heritage – Removing Art from Land and Historic Buildings' by Richard Harwood QC, Catherine Dobson, David Sawtell |
| 'The Limits of Separate Legal Personality: When Those Running a Company Can Be Held Personally Liable for Losses Caused to Third Parties Outside of the Company' by Dr Mike Wilkinson |
| 'A Practical Guide to Transgender Law' by Robin Moira White & Nicola Newbegin |
| 'Artificial Intelligence – The Practical Legal Issues (2nd Edition)' by John Buyers |
| 'A Practical Guide to Residential Freehold Conveyancing' by Lorraine Richardson |
| 'A Practical Guide to Pensions on Divorce for Lawyers' by Bryan Scant |
| 'A Practical Guide to Challenging Sham Marriage Allegations in Immigration Law' by Priya Solanki |
| 'A Practical Guide to Legal Rights in Scotland' by Sarah-Jane Macdonald |
| 'A Practical Guide to New Build Conveyancing' by Paul Sams & Rebecca East |
| 'A Practical Guide to Defending Barristers in Disciplinary Cases' by Marc Beaumont |
| 'A Practical Guide to Inherited Wealth on Divorce' by Hayley Trim |
| 'A Practical Guide to Practice Direction 12J and Domestic Abuse in Private Law Children Proceedings' by Rebecca Cross & Malvika Jaganmohan |
| 'A Practical Guide to Confiscation and Restraint' by Narita Bahra QC, John Carl Townsend, David Winch |
| 'A Practical Guide to the Law of Forests in Scotland' by Philip Buchan |
| 'A Practical Guide to Health and Medical Cases in Immigration Law' by Rebecca Chapman & Miranda Butler |
| 'A Practical Guide to Bad Character Evidence for Criminal Practitioners by Aparna Rao |
| 'A Practical Guide to Extradition Law post-Brexit' by Myles Grandison et al |

| |
|---|
| 'A Practical Guide to Hoarding and Mental Health for Housing Lawyers' by Rachel Coyle |
| 'A Practical Guide to Psychiatric Claims in Personal Injury – 2nd Edition' by Liam Ryan |
| 'Stephens on Contractual Indemnities' by Richard Stephens |
| 'A Practical Guide to the EU Succession Regulation' by Richard Frimston |
| 'A Practical Guide to Solicitor and Client Costs – 2nd Edition' by Robin Dunne |
| 'Constructive Dismissal – Practice Pointers and Principles' by Benjimin Burgher |
| 'A Practical Guide to Religion and Belief Discrimination Claims in the Workplace' by Kashif Ali |
| 'A Practical Guide to the Law of Medical Treatment Decisions' by Ben Troke |
| 'Fundamental Dishonesty and QOCS in Personal Injury Proceedings: Law and Practice' by Jake Rowley |
| 'A Practical Guide to the Law in Relation to School Exclusions' by Charlotte Hadfield & Alice de Coverley |
| 'A Practical Guide to Divorce for the Silver Separators' by Karin Walker |
| 'The Right to be Forgotten – The Law and Practical Issues' by Melissa Stock |
| 'A Practical Guide to Planning Law and Rights of Way in National Parks, the Broads and AONBs' by James Maurici QC, James Neill et al |
| 'A Practical Guide to Election Law' by Tom Tabori |
| 'A Practical Guide to the Law in Relation to Surrogacy' by Andrew Powell |
| 'A Practical Guide to Claims Arising from Fatal Accidents – 2nd Edition' by James Patience |
| 'A Practical Guide to the Ownership of Employee Inventions – From Entitlement to Compensation' by James Tumbridge & Ashley Roughton |
| 'A Practical Guide to Asbestos Claims' by Jonathan Owen & Gareth McAloon |
| 'A Practical Guide to Stamp Duty Land Tax in England and Northern Ireland' by Suzanne O'Hara |
| 'A Practical Guide to the Law of Farming Partnerships' by Philip Whitcomb |
| 'Covid-19, Homeworking and the Law – The Essential Guide to Employment and GDPR Issues' by Forbes Solicitors |
| 'Covid-19 and Criminal Law – The Essential Guide' by Ramya Nagesh |
| 'Covid-19 and Family Law in England and Wales – The Essential Guide' by Safda Mahmood |

| |
|---|
| 'A Practical Guide to the Law of Unlawful Eviction and Harassment – 2nd Edition' by Stephanie Lovegrove |
| 'Covid-19, Brexit and the Law of Commercial Leases – The Essential Guide' by Mark Shelton |
| 'A Practical Guide to Costs in Personal Injury Claims – 2nd Edition' by Matthew Hoe |
| 'A Practical Guide to the General Data Protection Regulation (GDPR) – 2nd Edition' by Keith Markham |
| 'Ellis on Credit Hire – Sixth Edition' by Aidan Ellis & Tim Kevan |
| 'A Practical Guide to Working with Litigants in Person and McKenzie Friends in Family Cases' by Stuart Barlow |
| 'Protecting Unregistered Brands: A Practical Guide to the Law of Passing Off' by Lorna Brazell |
| 'A Practical Guide to Secondary Liability and Joint Enterprise Post-Jogee' by Joanne Cecil & James Mehigan |
| 'A Practical Guide to the Pre-Action RTA Claims Protocol for Personal Injury Lawyers' by Antonia Ford |
| 'A Practical Guide to Neighbour Disputes and the Law' by Alexander Walsh |
| 'A Practical Guide to Forfeiture of Leases' by Mark Shelton |
| 'A Practical Guide to Coercive Control for Legal Practitioners and Victims' by Rachel Horman |
| 'A Practical Guide to Rights Over Airspace and Subsoil' by Daniel Gatty |
| 'Tackling Disclosure in the Criminal Courts – A Practitioner's Guide' by Narita Bahra QC & Don Ramble |
| 'A Practical Guide to the Law of Driverless Cars – Second Edition' by Alex Glassbrook, Emma Northey & Scarlett Milligan |
| 'A Practical Guide to TOLATA Claims' by Greg Williams |
| 'A Practical Guide to Elderly Law – 2nd Edition' by Justin Patten |
| 'A Practical Guide to Responding to Housing Disrepair and Unfitness Claims' by Iain Wightwick |
| 'A Practical Guide to the Construction and Rectification of Wills and Trust Instruments' by Edward Hewitt |
| 'A Practical Guide to the Law of Bullying and Harassment in the Workplace' by Philip Hyland |
| 'How to Be a Freelance Solicitor: A Practical Guide to the SRA-Regulated Freelance Solicitor Model' by Paul Bennett |

| |
|---|
| 'A Practical Guide to Prison Injury Claims' by Malcolm Johnson |
| 'A Practical Guide to the Small Claims Track - 2nd Edition' by Dominic Bright |
| 'A Practical Guide to Advising Clients at the Police Station' by Colin Stephen McKeown-Beaumont |
| 'A Practical Guide to Antisocial Behaviour Injunctions' by Iain Wightwick |
| 'Practical Mediation: A Guide for Mediators, Advocates, Advisers, Lawyers, and Students in Civil, Commercial, Business, Property, Workplace, and Employment Cases' by Jonathan Dingle with John Sephton |
| 'The Mini-Pupillage Workbook' by David Boyle |
| 'A Practical Guide to Crofting Law' by Brian Inkster |
| 'A Practical Guide to Spousal Maintenance' by Liz Cowell |
| 'A Practical Guide to the Law of Domain Names and Cybersquatting' by Andrew Clemson |
| 'A Practical Guide to the Law of Gender Pay Gap Reporting' by Harini Iyengar |
| 'A Practical Guide to the Rights of Grandparents in Children Proceedings' by Stuart Barlow |
| 'NHS Whistleblowing and the Law' by Joseph England |
| 'Employment Law and the Gig Economy' by Nigel Mackay & Annie Powell |
| 'A Practical Guide to Noise Induced Hearing Loss (NIHL) Claims' by Andrew Mckie, Ian Skeate, Gareth McAloon |
| 'An Introduction to Beauty Negligence Claims – A Practical Guide for the Personal Injury Practitioner' by Greg Almond |
| 'Intercompany Agreements for Transfer Pricing Compliance' by Paul Sutton |
| 'Zen and the Art of Mediation' by Martin Plowman |
| 'A Practical Guide to the SRA Principles, Individual and Law Firm Codes of Conduct 2019 – What Every Law Firm Needs to Know' by Paul Bennett |
| 'A Practical Guide to Adoption for Family Lawyers' by Graham Pegg |
| 'A Practical Guide to Industrial Disease Claims' by Andrew Mckie & Ian Skeate |
| 'A Practical Guide to Redundancy' by Philip Hyland |
| 'A Practical Guide to Vicarious Liability' by Mariel Irvine |
| 'A Practical Guide to Applications for Landlord's Consent and Variation of Leases' by Mark Shelton |
| 'A Practical Guide to Relief from Sanctions Post-Mitchell and Denton' by Peter Causton |

| | |
|---|---|
| 'A Practical Guide to Equity Release for Advisors' by Paul Sams | |
| 'A Practical Guide to Financial Services Claims' by Chris Hegarty | |
| 'The Law of Houses in Multiple Occupation: A Practical Guide to HMO Proceedings' by Julian Hunt | |
| 'Occupiers, Highways and Defective Premises Claims: A Practical Guide Post-Jackson – 2nd Edition' by Andrew Mckie | |
| 'A Practical Guide to Financial Ombudsman Service Claims' by Adam Temple & Robert Scrivenor | |
| 'A Practical Guide to Advising Schools on Employment Law' by Jonathan Holden | |
| 'A Practical Guide to Running Housing Disrepair and Cavity Wall Claims: 2nd Edition' by Andrew Mckie & Ian Skeate | |
| 'A Practical Guide to Holiday Sickness Claims – 2nd Edition' by Andrew Mckie & Ian Skeate | |
| 'Arguments and Tactics for Personal Injury and Clinical Negligence Claims' by Dorian Williams | |
| 'A Practical Guide to Drone Law' by Rufus Ballaster, Andrew Firman, Eleanor Clot | |
| 'A Practical Guide to Compliance for Personal Injury Firms Working With Claims Management Companies' by Paul Bennett | |
| 'RTA Allegations of Fraud in a Post-Jackson Era: The Handbook – 2nd Edition' by Andrew Mckie | |
| 'RTA Personal Injury Claims: A Practical Guide Post-Jackson' by Andrew Mckie | |
| 'On Experts: CPR35 for Lawyers and Experts' by David Boyle | |
| 'An Introduction to Personal Injury Law' by David Boyle | |

These books and more are available to order online direct from the publisher at www.lawbriefpublishing.com, where you can also read free sample chapters. For any queries, contact us on 0844 587 2383 or mail@lawbriefpublishing.com.

Our books are also usually in stock at www.amazon.co.uk with free next day delivery for Prime members, and at good legal bookshops such as Wildy & Sons.

We are regularly launching new books in our series of practical day-to-day practitioners' guides. Visit our website and join our free newsletter to be kept informed and to receive special offers, free chapters, etc.

You can also follow us on Twitter at www.twitter.com/lawbriefpub.